The Unrandom Universe

Sigmund Brouwer

HARVEST HOUSE PUBLISHERS
Eugene, Oregon 97402

Illustrations by Michael W. Carroll

Cover by Left Coast Design, Portland, Oregon

THE UNRANDOM UNIVERSE
Copyright © 2002 by Sigmund Brouwer
Published by Harvest House Publishers
Eugene, Oregon 97402

Library of Congress Cataloging-in-Publication Data
  Brouwer, Sigmund, 1959–
      The unrandom universe / Sigmund Brouwer
         p. cm.
      Includes bibliographical references.
      ISBN 0-7369-0295-3
      1. Religion and science. I. Title.
  BL240.3.B76 2002
  261.5'5—dc21   2001051578

Printed in the United States of America

02 03 04 05 06 07 / VP-CF / 10 9 8 7 6 5 4 3 2 1

Contents

1
The Face of God

The heavens tell of the glory of God. The skies display his marvelous craftsmanship. Day after day they continue to speak; night after night they make him known. They speak without a sound or a word; their voice is silent in the skies; yet their message has gone out to all the earth, and their words to all the world.

PSALM 19:1-4

Because I am writing this book in first person, it probably alerts you to the fact that although this is a book about science, it is not, strictly speaking, a science book. Instead, it is the reflections of a personal search.

In fact, I would like early to make it clear that my academic background is in journalism, not science. My total claim to an *official* science lies in first- and second-year university courses in chemistry, biology, and genetics—enough to allow me a sense of the fascination at the workings of nature, and certainly enough for me to understand and deeply respect the work, devotion, and applied intelligence that scientific disciplines require of those who enter the field. We on the outside rarely know how much gratitude we owe our scientists for their personal sacrifices in advancing human knowledge.

Since I am not qualified as a scientist to represent any discipline of science, let alone a spectrum of disciplines, my fear is that writing *The Unrandom Universe* will be seen as an audacious act. The only way I can justify it is to ask that this book be read in the spirit it is offered: as a conversation, hopefully lively, interesting, and thought-provoking.

The qualification, however, that I do offer is my background as an author. I would argue that—whether nonfiction or novels—an author's task is simple: to serve as a conduit, to take what we learn about the world and present it as truly as we can. Which is not to say that I or other authors always succeed, only that we must try, and that collectively, our voices do help make some sense of the world around us. (Much more of this self-serving philosophy and I'll have to wear a tweed jacket and smoke a pipe and stare thoughtfully into the distance as I pose for the obligatory back-cover photo.)

In the early 1990s—doesn't that already sound so last-century?—I began to read as much as I could about genetics, intrigued at some of the fascinating fiction possibilities. Although some geneticists disagreed, others at that time boldly predicted that within 20 to 30 years it just might be possible to clone a mammal. Armed accordingly by what I learned, I wrote one of the first speculative novels on the subject, *Double Helix,* about a scientist trying to clone humans, using this fiction to explore some of the real-life implications of DNA research. Two years after *Double Helix* was published—not 20 or 30—I was astounded to open a newspaper to the headlines about a Scottish scientist who introduced Dolly the sheep to the world. Cloning had arrived. By the end of the decade, human cloning had moved from speculative fiction to a threatened reality. While I am grateful for Dolly—thanks to her, *Double Helix* briefly resurfaced on a best-seller list—I was indignant and amused four years after publication of *Double Helix* when I saw an amazon.com reader's review refer to the novel as an "unsophisticated and over-worn plot regarding human cloning." This says much about the rapid speed of modern scientific advances; in less than a decade, cloning had gone from science fiction to science fact to science cliché.

I wrote a more recent novel, *Out of the Shadows*, using an astronomer to tell the story first person, an astronomer who grudgingly begins to see God because of what he learns in the night skies. To write as that fictional character, I had to learn as much as I could about astronomy, and it was through this background research that I first wondered about attempting *The Unrandom Universe;* learning more about astronomy reconfirmed for me that science is not an enemy of faith in God.

During the writing of *Double Helix*, I had spoken with genetic scientists who could not escape the conclusion that DNA is a product of intelligent design of some sort of Supreme Being; as background research for *Out of the Shadows*, I found that some astronomers were prepared to use their science to argue the same thing about the origins of the universe. More astounding to me was discovering that there were even those who believed that science pointed us to the conclusion that the entire 15- to 18-billion-year evolution of the universe was designed to create mankind.

I hope this book serves, then, as a conduit of what I have learned in preparation for those novels and in my extended readings since. Some of it you may know already, and some of it may be as new to you as it was to me.

I hope, too, some readers find that this conversation—unfortunately one-sided because of the nature of reading—will strengthen their faith in a God who created us. I hope other readers, who are willing to speculate about God's existence, will see that there is much reason for a reasoning person to believe that He created us.

I would like to be careful to point out that I have done no scientific research, aside from reading about those discoveries and marveling at what scientists have uncovered in their respective disciplines of science.

I must also be careful to add that I came to this book—and indeed all my reading of scientific discoveries—with a foundational belief that I live in a universe created by a God who, despite all our flaws, loves us as we love our own children.

This foundational belief may seem to have a lack of objectivity. Far from it. Learning more about science became a test of my faith, for I was my own devil's advocate. Every step of this journey, I examined what science told me against what I knew and believed about God. I confess that as the journey began, I was anxiously afraid I would find something in science that would make it impossible for me to sustain faith in a God behind this universe.

I found the opposite.

To those readers who question the existence of God, my perceived lack of objectivity may seem unfair to take into a book-long argument that this universe is not a random act.

My counterpoint is that it appears that, for the most part, "objective" science precludes considering the existence of God. At this point it is no longer objective, for it begins with a premise and, in direct contradiction to the hallowed scientific method, does not test it.

In humanity's search for truth, why *not* put God back into scientific discussions?

If God did not create the universe, a search in science for Him will show nothing to suggest a supernatural Creator.

If God created this universe, however, God is behind all science. While scientific proof of His existence may be beyond our capabilities, at the very least, science should point to His existence.

Thus, in your search for truth, it is entirely fair to openly consider what science has to tell us about the existence of a supernatural Creator, and then accept or reject His existence.

Like me, you may be surprised to find out how much science will test determined skepticism in God.

And how much it can strengthen faith.

Any argument requires ground rules. Here are mine.

First, this is a book about the existence of God, not a theological discussion on who He is, or how you should relate to God, or how He relates to us. While I believe there is much beyond acknowledging His existence that is profoundly important to our souls, I simply hope this serves as a beginning or continuation to a lifelong spiritual search of understanding God. Some in science refer to the Creator as the Supreme Being; because of my faith background, I prefer to refer to Him as God, with all the respect and awe that I can give.

Second, this book largely discusses western thought over the last millennium, based on a Judeo-Christian perspective. There may be readers who rightly question why eastern views on religion are ignored along with ancient Arabic or Chinese science—both at different times far more advanced than western science. My answer is that I focus on the modern science of the last five centuries, and, broadly speaking, this science and its method of experimentation largely sprang from the European Renaissance with its Judeo-Christian base. (Which is not to suggest that those scientists ignored all that had been learned before them in the other cultures.)

Third, I sometimes refer to and assume two camps of thought that traditionally have been perceived as being at odds with the other: religion and science. On one side of the divide, there are those who do not want to face any faith doubts created by scientists. On the other are those in science who fuel the doubt, intentionally or not. I would like to make it clear this is a historical generalization, for many with faith in God embrace science, and many scientists embrace faith in God.

There is no reason for the divide.

Both sides are concerned with seeking truth.

And truth, if it is truth, is indivisible.

This is something I believe each of us will understand much more fully beyond this life.

Finally, I do not dispute the accepted data and facts of the different disciplines of science.

I only mention this because, as an example, I have read and heard of people who insist the age of the Earth should be measured in thousands of years, and claim that dinosaur bones have been planted by the devil to deceive us and remove our faith. (To them, science is convenient when it brings electricity into their homes, powering televisions built because of the accumulation of scientific knowledge, so that they can view satellite-beamed programming of television preachers who vilify the evils of science.)

I accept this data because I don't have the time or knowledge to verify the distance to the sun or the way that DNA replicates or the behavior of electrons at a nuclear level as shown in particle accelerators. But I can and will learn from those who have or can verify the facts presented. These scientists are men and women who should be respected for their intelligence and integrity; broadly speaking, one scientist's data, whether it is centuries old or this month's, is not accepted unless other scientists can verify it under similar experimental conditions.

This does not mean, however, that the *conclusions* for this data are something any of us should accept blindly or

R. Williams and the HDF Team (ST ScI) and NASA

Hubble telescope's deepest-ever view of the universe

without question. Data and conclusions are vastly different creatures. That is why there are often so many disputes in the scientific world; the interpretation of data generates volumes of argument.

(In an ideal world, our children would clearly understand this difference as they receive their educations. There is a condoned unfairness about atheist science teachers who use scientific data to enforce a specific worldview upon young students too inexperienced to realize inarguable data can lead to arguable conclusions. Nor is it fair that only the atheist view is presented. It wasn't until I was long out of school, for example, that I discovered many of the greatest scientists—Galileo and Newton, to name two—were men of great faith in a God behind this universe.)

Given that facts and data of science can lead different scientists to different conclusions, I do think it is fair to consider that science shows that God—however each of us might understand Him—created us.

While the goal of this book is to show how science and faith are not at odds, by definition, faith is not a matter of knowledge and applied intellectual reason.

Yet knowledge and reason need not be obstacles to faith. Especially not scientific knowledge.

Albert Einstein's unequaled scientific genius gave him a perspective on matters of science beyond the comprehension of any of us.

"The scientist is possessed by the sense of universal causation," Einstein wrote. "His religious feeling takes the form of a rapturous amazement at the harmony of natural law, which reveals an intelligence of such superiority that, compared with it, all the systematic thinking and acting of human beings is an utterly insignificant reflection."

If his genius brought him close to the face of God, the rest of us, possessed of far lesser vision, are still able to take great comfort in what Einstein saw.

2

Cosmic Debris?

And the Lord God formed a man's body from
the dust of the ground and breathed into it the
breath of life.

GENESIS 2:7

In the short time it takes you to finish reading the first sentence of this chapter, the medium-sized star at the hub of our solar system will convert 2,400 million tons of hydrogen into 2,384 million tons of helium, spewing light and X-rays into all directions of the infinite vacuum that surrounds it. This newly created energy will reach our Earth in just over eight minutes, where our atmosphere will absorb a fraction of it. The rest of the energy, which we see as light, will continue outward from the sun as it travels at 186,000 miles per second on an infinite journey to the edge of an expanding universe.

For a moment, set aside trying to comprehend the billions of years that our sun has burned and will continue to burn at this equally incomprehensible rate of consumption. Set aside the fact that our sun is one of trillions of stars, all spewing energy into the void. Set aside the fact that our sun is normal to the point of boring; and set aside the fact that beyond the solar system exist giant stars with enough gravity to rip our sun into a ghostly shroud millions of miles across, dead stars collapsed into black holes capable of swallowing all light and material of entire solar systems, and supernovas that briefly light entire corners of the universe.

Instead, consider that all these stellar glories lead to the profoundly simple yet disturbing paradox that humans have grappled with since the first of us looked upward into a night sky: either there was a beginning point in which this vast amount of cosmic substance came into being, or it has forever existed in one form or another.

Both propositions are impossible.

Nothing in our material universe can exist without a fixed starting point in time.

Nor can all this cosmic substance spring into existence from nothingness.

Both propositions are impossible in a natural system.

Yet stars and the rest of the universe do exist.

As do we.

In trying to understand the beginnings of this universe, the evidence of cosmic science also shows us the remarkable manner in which the sun produces energy.

Here on Earth, we watch a log in the fire disappear or the needle on the gas gauge lower, and we intuitively understand that energy is produced by a destruction of sorts. Complex hydrocarbon molecules break down into simpler components, and at a chemical level, energy is a by-product of this destruction.

To picture this process—although it is not an entirely accurate analogy—imagine a hammer coming down with enough force to smash a steel ball into hundreds of smaller balls. At the nuclear level of elements such as uranium, for example, the process is called *fission*. The tremendous force unleashed provides the awesome destructive power of atomic weapons, or the energy production of nuclear plants.

Stars, however, generate energy in an opposite way, through nuclear *fusion*. Using the same analogy, imagine smaller balls gathered together and squeezed into each other to form a single, larger ball. If the balls are made of soft damp clay, any of us can do it with the pressure of our hands. The pressure and heat required to fuse smaller steel balls into a larger one, of course, is much greater than what we are capable of with muscles and ligaments, and this fusing requires the energy given by a blast furnace and tongs.

At a subatomic level, it takes the forces of gravity in the mind-boggling mass of a star to provide the mind-boggling heat and pressure capable of fusing simpler elements into more complex ones. Thus, in nuclear fusion, energy is released as hydrogen is fused into helium. Eventually, this helium begins to fuse into lithium, and so on.

Over the billions of years since the beginning of time, as the evidence of science tells us, this process of fusion converted the primary elements in the universe—hydrogen, helium, lithium—into all the elements that now exist. Different compounds of the resulting elements now form the complexity of materials around us.

Stars are too small to create complex elements beyond iron. During the intense heat of their explosion, massive stars that become supernovas create all the more complex elements and spew them out into the universe.

As science today understands it, then, our planet and everything on it and in it, every molecule of each of our bodies, from hydrocarbons of protein and fat and other tissues to trace elements to water itself, is literally made from scattered cosmic debris.

This is strictly an aside thought: since fusion is possible through the force provided by gravity, indirectly then, stars convert gravity into usable energy and disperse it throughout the universe.

Thus, it can be said that gravity is the foundational source of all energy.

Scientists, although they can measure and predict the effects of gravity, have no explanation for why gravity exists or how it works.

The ancients gave us the Genesis account long before scientists gave us the big bang theory and the theories of the birth and evolution of stars and explanations of nuclear physics. Yet even without this scientific knowledge, the ancients were able to simply and elegantly express the cosmic truth of our existence:

Our human bodies are formed "from the dust of the ground."

Modern cosmology, then, verifies this wisdom of the ancients. Had the ancients simply begun or stopped there, no scientist could dispute that portion of the seventh verse of the second chapter of Genesis.

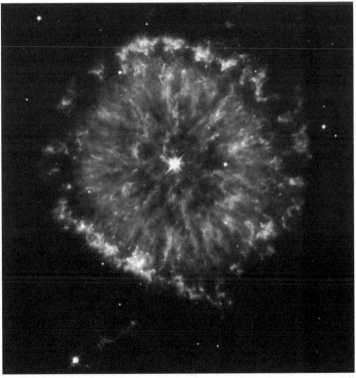

NASA

Planetary nebula NGC 6751

The most profound aspect of human existence lies in the remainder of what the ancients declared (my emphasis added):

"*And the Lord God* formed a man's body from the dust of the ground *and breathed into it the breath of life.*"

Did the ancients claim that a giant being—God—squatted on this planet and molded a little figurine from dirt or clay, then blew some breath into the figurine and watched it come to life as a human? While there are those who might disagree, I would argue there is nothing about the language of that statement to suggest such a fundamental and literal interpretation.

Yet the verse shines with truth.

Given their understanding of the world around them and their lack of modern scientific terms, the ancients tell us—with that language of wonderful simplicity and elegance—that God, by some method outside our perceived laws of nature, created all life, including ours as humans.

And that is the core issue: the foundation of human existence, upon which every personal philosophy must rest. Were we created with a soul engineered for union with that God in this life and beyond? Or are we simply cosmic debris belched forth from the stars, the product of a random universe?

3

The Great Divide

I believe the intention of Holy Writ was to persuade men of the truths necessary for salvation, such as neither science nor any other means could render credible, but only the voice of the Holy Spirit. But I do not think it necessary to believe that the same God who gave us our senses, our speech, our intellect, would have put aside the use of these, to teach us instead such things as with their help we could find out for ourselves, particularly in the case of these sciences of which there is not the smallest mention in the Scriptures; and, above all, in astronomy, of which so little notice is taken that the names of none of the planets are mentioned. Surely if the intention of the sacred scribes had been to teach the people astronomy, they would not have passed over the subject so completely.[1]

GALILEO GALILEI, 1613 A.D

Random universe?

Or unrandom?

Over the last five centuries, as mankind's scientific knowledge increased dramatically, an immense divide grew between those two apparently opposite and irreconcilable views. The more we understood about science, the more it seemed unnecessary to include God as part of the clock-work process of the running of the universe; the more it seemed ridiculous to try to insert Him into our understanding of the universe; and the more it seemed difficult to hold onto faith in God against the opposition of the proven claims of science.

This scientific climate, in essence, led to naturalism, for it seemed that the laws of the universe gave simple, natural explanations for how things work. The explanation for our existence could be found in science alone. We are here, the scientific world told us in naturalism, simply because we are here. Furthermore, understanding the laws of the universe is enough to understand how we got here.

This naturalism was in direct contradiction to the supernatural claims of the Bible. For people of intellectual reason, God was not the reason for nature, but nature just existed. Without God. The myths of religious faith were simply manufactured to comfort people of lesser intelligence.

This was and is the divide.

An entire chapter devoted indirectly to some science history—and more directly to the history of a divide between science and religion—may seem unnecessary and inapplicable to any personal faith search.

But understanding the history teaches us three strong and worthwhile lessons.

The first is a harsh one to those of faith in God. Without sound scientific knowledge, it is difficult to respond intelligently to skeptics who use science to question the biblical claims of a supernatural Creator.

The second lesson is comforting to those of faith who take the effort to understand science. In his book *The Science of God*, distinguished physicist and biblical scholar Gerald Schroeder points out that if you avoid a subjective bending of the Bible to match science, or of science to match the Bible, faith does not require faith alone. Science is a strong ally.

And the third lesson comes with understanding the pointlessness of the battles that have created this divide between science and faith. It is best summed up by the medieval philosopher Moses Maimonides, who wrote that conflicts between science and the Bible result from one of two things: a lack of scientific knowledge, or a defective understanding of the Bible.

I am probably not alone when I admit that my childhood education led me to mistakenly believe that science and religion were at odds. For example, I thought that in his showdown against the church, Galileo had been right and the Bible had been wrong. I felt that to cling to faith, I, like the church, needed to reject what was seemingly undeniable about science. Well into my university years, where I received science instruction from atheist professors, this misperception left me guilty of an inarticulate doubt I dared not admit, not even to myself.

When I discovered more about the sources of my mis-perceptions, I finally understood. The battle is not between the truths of science and religion, but between scientists and nonscientists, and too often between scientists and religious leaders.

I have not devoted a lifetime to understanding science. Nor have I exhaustively studied the Bible, let alone the Hebrew and Greek languages that give more illumination to its passages.

I know I am an expert in neither.

Understanding our deficiencies, however, gives any of us a certain strength that comes with an ability not to make knee-jerk assumptions about either science or the Bible. A searching open mind leads to illumination; determined ignorance leads to mistrust, mistrust to enmity.

A theologian with decades of study who assumes that reading articles in the popular press provides enough knowledge to evaluate the validity of scientific discoveries is as guilty of this evil ignorance as a scientist at the top of his field who assumes that a simple reading of the Bible is enough to acquire biblical wisdom.

With the arrogance of assumed knowledge, meaningful discussion between both those sides is impossible, no matter how committed each might be to finding truth. When their disagreements become public fights—I am about to describe the most infamous ones—it badly distorts truth for the spectators, those of us with genuine curiosity but expertise in neither field.

This harm spills from one generation to the next. And continues for centuries.

Roger Bacon, the celebrated thirteenth-century scientist, studied the properties of light and rainbows and described the process for making gunpowder; the religious establishment accused him of black magic, and he could not convince Pope Clement IV to admit experimental sciences to university curriculum. In the centuries that followed, church leaders would view other scientists with equal suspicion. By the time Nicolaus Copernicus had the audacity to disagree with the religious establishment and propose that the sun was at the center of our solar system, the tension between religion and science was primed for an all-out brawl.

Enter Galileo Galilei, the Italian astronomer and physicist.

Born in 1564, Galileo is often viewed as the scientist most responsible for the great divide between religion and science. Ironically, as the quote at the beginning of this chapter shows, Galileo was a man of deep faith whose attitude was that of a Vatican librarian of his time—the Bible is a book about how one goes to heaven, not about how heaven goes.

While Galileo didn't invent the telescope—another common misperception—he improved its design and turned it heavenward. What he saw was the first clear evidence that Aristotle and Ptolemy had been wrong to claim the Earth was at the center of the universe. Copernicus, it was obvious, had been right in his theory about the movement of the planets.

As a man supportive of the Catholic Church, Galileo also saw something else. Soon, very soon, because of the telescope and its spread to other scientists across Europe, the leaders in Rome would be proven wrong if they continued to proclaim Copernicus's theory as heresy.

Unlike some of those church leaders, Galileo's strong faith in God was not shaken by his discovery. (Nor, in retrospect, should ours be. Does the Earth's location have any relevance to belief in a Creator of the universe? For that matter, nowhere does the Bible claim that the Earth is central to anything, especially given that Earth takes second place in the first sentence of the Bible—"In the beginning God created the heavens and the earth.") To help his friends in the church, Galileo wrote a letter to show that Copernicus's theory was indeed consistent with Catholic doctrine and correct interpretation of the Bible. The church, he basically stated, should revise its stand.

Mistake. Not his letter, but his perception of how it would be received.

Galileo had just as many enemies as friends in the church, for he had a quick wit and a quicker impatience with those who could not follow or agree with his science. More unfortunate was the political climate at the time, characterized by the power held by the church's Inquisition, a committee dedicated to seeking and punishing heretics. In 1616 A.D., his enemies pulled enough political strings that Galileo was summoned to Rome to defend his letter. He was cleared of the charges of heresy and allowed

Galileo may have seen a view much like this on the first night he spotted Jupiter's four moons

to treat the Copernican theory as hypothetical, but not true. Nonetheless, Galileo was ordered not to "hold or defend" the Copernican theory again. (This marked ambivalence of the Inquisition shows, I think, that even within the church there were those who saw no reason for a divide between religion and science.)

Sixteen years later, Galileo tried to walk that tightrope of discussing the "hypothetical" theory without declaring it true. He did so in a book now hailed as a scientific masterpiece, *Dialogue Concerning the Two Chief World Systems*. He compared Ptolemaic-Aristotelian theory to Copernican theory, merely emphasizing the logical superiority of the second system, without necessarily declaring it to be true. His carefully chosen semantics wasn't a good enough balancing act on that tightrope; his book was enough for his enemies in the church to bring him back to Rome for charges of heresy.

In defense of the church, the validity of Galileo's science was not on trial. (According to official transcripts of the trial, it was never even debated.) To his shrewd and gleeful enemies, the truth of Galileo's arguments was irrelevant against the undeniable fact that Galileo had disobeyed the previous order not to "hold or defend" the Copernican theory.

The result is what I learned in childhood without understanding the politics behind it. Galileo was found guilty as charged; while it was unlikely he would have been executed, against the threat of such punishment, he chose to publicly withdraw his statement, then was betrayed by receiving life imprisonment as punishment anyway. This he served in the relative comfort of house arrest in a Florence villa.

But the damage was done. His book was out there, and the controversy only made it more popular. (Things in the publishing world don't change. Someone, please, hold a book-burning party and invite the press to watch you burn this one. Sales will jump tremendously.)

In Galileo's case, science had proven the stand of the church wrong, the church lost its monopoly on "truth," and since then religion has been perceived as antiscience.[2]

A historical summary of this event allows us too easily to ignore the human drama. Galileo was the first to discover four moons circling Jupiter and the first to see that the moon was not perfect, but mountainous and pitted. Can you imagine his excitement as he explored the solar system? His joy to be engaged in pursuit of truth? His sorrow, outrage, and exhaustion as the church fought him in his old age and finally forced him to recant?

Here is, I believe, the most important and most forgotten point about Galileo's trial:

Galileo's verified scientific data had no dispute with the Bible. Nor against the existence of God.

The dispute arose because of the non-biblical claims of church leaders—who were not scientists themselves.

Yet when the church leaders were proven to be fools, it was—and still is—widely perceived that science was right and religion was wrong.

The advice of Maimonides bears repeating: conflicts between science and the Bible result from a lack of scientific knowledge or a defective understanding of the Bible.

In the trial against Galileo, the church leaders were fully guilty of both.

As this shows, misguided defenders of faith—religious leaders or laypeople—who stray onto scientific turf without scientific knowledge are easily mocked when easily proven wrong.

This is one reason that many of faith, like the historic church leaders, view science with suspicion.

The famous German astronomer Johannes Kepler (1571–1630) was a committed Christian with a brilliant scientific mind. His discovery that the orbits of the planets were elliptical rather than a perfect circle disturbed the religious establishment of his time. Circles were perfect, the establishment proposed, as was God. Therefore, they reasoned, God would only make circular orbits, not defective elliptical ones.

This was not a claim based on biblical knowledge, but rather on an assumption made by religious leaders on the behalf of God.

It is no surprise, then, when those in science regard those in the church with equal suspicion.

Another infamous example adding to the perception of science/right and religion/wrong is the estimate of the age of the universe by James Ussher, an Irish archbishop who died in 1656.

Ussher, not a scientist by any means, summed the generations listed in the Hebrew Bible. Estimating the reigns of the various rulers and tallying backwards, he boldly proclaimed that the world had been created at high noon on October 23, 4004 B.C.

Ussher—a clergyman, not a scientist—used the Bible as a scientific tool to calculate a 6,000-year-old universe. His action and claim is often scorned today, with the implication that it is representative of the divide between "true" science and "foolish" religion.

Scorners, however, should keep in mind that while the before-mentioned Kepler, a top scientist of that day, did disagree with Ussher, Kepler simply argued for a spring creation date instead of autumn!

Furthermore, until widespread acceptance of the big bang theory a few decades ago, the majority of astronomers and physicists believed in an infinitely old steady state universe. With new astronomical evidence in the last four decades, the Genesis claim to a beginning point of the universe has been dramatically validated.

So here's the irony of a Genesis-based claim about creation: While the 6,000 years declared by Ussher and Kepler is drastically different than the now estimated 15- to 18-billion-year age of the universe, it's still infinitely closer to correct than what most scientists believed until near the end of the twentieth century.

If Galileo's fight with the Catholic Church marks the beginning of science's triumph over religion, a much more modern trial served, in the public eye, as a final coronation of the victor.

Dayton, Tennessee, 1924. A former presidential candidate on one side. A famous criminal lawyer on the other. A high school teacher in the middle, backed by the American Civil Liberties Union (ACLU). Evolution versus the Bible. Reason against faith.

And faith seemed to lose badly.

They called it the "monkey trial." Along with the televised spectacle of O.J. Simpson and Johnny Cochran, the Scopes Trial is one of the most famous and controversial American legal battles of the American twentieth century.

The short of it is very simple. Tennessee had passed a law banning the teaching of the relatively new theory of evolution; John Thomas Scopes, the high school teacher, was charged with breaking the law by discussing this theory in the classroom. The case might have passed into obscurity except for the participation of the ACLU, which wanted to challenge the law as a violation of the constitutional principle of the separation of church and state. What raised the stakes even higher was the additional participation of William Jennings Bryan, who aided the prosecution, and Clarence Darrow, who defended Scopes.

For the media, it was the perfect circus event, not only a showdown between religion and science, but also a showdown between two high-profile figures clearly on opposites sides.

Bryan had run for president three times, was a well-known lecturer, was considered an expert on the Bible, and believed in fundamentalism, insisting every word in the Bible should be taken literally.

Darrow, the most famous American lawyer of the early 1900s, known worldwide as a brilliant criminal defender, believed strongly in the right to teach evolution.

Yet technically, Darrow could mount no defense. His client, Scopes, had broken the law, whether that law was right or wrong. There was no denying Scopes had taught evolution to his students. Darrow undoubtedly knew this and planned his defense like a chess game.

The impact of the trial on public consciousness resulted from Darrow's canny move to challenge Bryan to take the stand as a witness on behalf of the Bible's view of creation. When Bryan foolishly accepted, Darrow had succeeded in moving the focus of the trial to an area that no amount of debate has definitively settled—the truth of evolution versus creationism.

Imagine your glee as a reporter to watch a former presidential candidate skewered on the witness stand.

For Bryan would have done well to decline Darrow's challenge, to heed that centuries-old admonition of Maimonides: conflicts between science and the Bible result from a lack of scientific knowledge or a defective understanding of the Bible.

Bryan was hampered by a lack of scientific knowledge, and in need of a more comprehensive understanding of the Bible. Furthermore, in Darrow, he faced one of the world's foremost trial lawyers, a lawyer protected in this debate by court rules, a lawyer intent on twisting and humiliating Bryan with word games, unanswerable questions, and the apparent contradictions of the Genesis account.

Here is one of the exchanges, which came as Bryan answered questions about the first days of creation in Genesis:

Darrow: "Have you any idea of the length of these periods?"

Bryan: "No; I don't."

Darrow: "Do you think the sun was made on the fourth day?"

Bryan: "Yes."

Darrow: "And they had evening and morning without the sun?"

Bryan: "I am simply saying it is a period."

Darrow: "They had evening and morning for four periods without the sun, do you think?"

Bryan: "I believe in creation as there told, and if I am not able to explain it I will accept it."

Few newspapers were as kind in reporting the trial as the Memphis *Commercial Appeal*, with an article that concluded: "It was not a contest. Consequently there was no victory. Darrow succeeded in showing that Bryan knows little about the science of the world. Bryan succeeded in bearing witness bravely to the faith which he believes transcends all the learning of men."

It was such a debacle that Bryan was not allowed on the witness stand the next day. The judge went as far as ordering his testimony expunged from the record, giving this ruling: "I feel that the testimony of Mr. Bryan can shed no light upon any issue that will be pending before a higher court; the issue now is whether or not Mr. Scopes taught that man descended from a lower order of animals."

To make all this more dramatic, and searing it further into public consciousness, William Jennings Bryan died in Dayton while resting after the trial.

The judge, of course, was correct. The trial was not about the veracity of evolution, but about a teacher who had broken a law that banned teaching it. Darrow lost the trial. Scopes was found guilty of teaching the theory of evolution.

The cultural result was far more reaching. Because Darrow had shifted the focus to a debate against a badly prepared and overconfident opponent, evolution, as represented by Darrow, came out the victor. Creationism, as represented by William Jennings Bryan, had no chance.

On the witness stand in court.

And in the media, where a jubilant liberal press portrayed all creationists as ignorant and badly out of touch with mainstream science.

The biggest impact in public consciousness, however, came from a wildly inaccurate retelling of the trial, a play called *Inherit the Wind.*

Even though the playwrights cautioned they were not pretending to be journalists, the caricatures they painted of the trial's participants became the ones that endured in public memory.

Here, the schoolteacher was seen dragged out of his classroom and into jail by a mob; in real life, the people of Dayton were polite. It was the defense who had insisted on taking the case to trial, and Scopes never faced jail.

Bryan, however, suffered more in the retelling. His character, Brady, is transformed into a mindless reactionary. As a representative of creationists, he is given lines that make him sound far more foolish than he did in real life. In the play, he opens his defense by insisting that God created in six 24-hour days, beginning "on the 23rd of October in the year 4004 B.C. at—uh, 9:00 A.M.!"

The play, in its time, was the longest-running drama on Broadway, then in the 1960s, became a hit movie starring Spencer Tracy and Gene Kelly. Inaccurate as it was historically, the movie version of *Inherit the Wind* became a popular teaching tool in classrooms.

Because most Americans learned about the trial in this manner, the impact of *Inherit the Wind* was far greater than that of the trial itself. Carl Sagan, who to millions represented science because of his television stature, said this: "The movie *Inherit the Wind* probably had a considerable national influence; it was the first time...that American movies made explicit the apparent contradictions and inconsistencies in the book of Genesis."

In the public consciousness, this impression has not changed in the decades since.

The truth that must be emphasized, however, is that creationism did not lose at the Scopes Trial.

Only the person who represented it.

Because the Bible was not written as a science manual, it is difficult to use the truths of the Bible to argue science.

But the truths of science provide a wonderful tool to argue the Bible. Because in those decades since the Scopes Trial, science has brought us incredible findings that do point toward the God who created an unrandom universe.

As Francis Bacon said, a little science estranges a man from God, but a lot of science brings him back.

4
Man Without God

First scene, outdoors at night:

Calvin: Look at all the stars! The universe just goes out forever and forever!

Hobbes: It kind of makes you wonder why man considers himself such a screaming big deal.

Following scene, indoors, as Calvin sits in a comfortable chair and points a remote control at the television:

Calvin to Hobbes: That's why we stay inside with our appliances.

BILL WATTERSON
One-page cartoon spread,
Calvin & Hobbes, *It's a Magical World*

Cartoonist Bill Watterson's commentary on modern America is a devastatingly wry implication that science without God leads to cynicism and a sense of life without meaning.

It wasn't always like this, of course.

Pre-Renaissance, mankind held all of nature in superstitious awe. During thunderstorms, the gods spoke. An eclipse of the sun was a sign from God. Plagues were divinely sent to punish.

Along with the fears inspired by scientific ignorance, poets and artists and scientists marveled and searched without embarrassment for the Creator who gave us life and the awareness to consider His existence.

Mankind shared the same wonder at the universe that Calvin blurts to his friend Hobbes.

"Look at all the stars. The universe just goes out for-ever and forever!"

Then came the European Renaissance. Starting with Galileo, when the church lost its monopoly on truth, religion—at first gradually, then cataclysmically—lost its iron grip on science and art.

Mysteries of nature that religion had attributed to the gods or to God at this point seemed to have simple mechanical explanations. We learned about the behavior of electricity, predicted the effects of gravity and the motions of the planets and stars, understood bacteria, probed the composition of atoms and molecules.

Over the last five centuries, Earth lost its place at the center of the universe. As did, eventually, the sun. And, finally, man. Through science, we began to believe the sunset on the horizon resulted from a mechanical, impersonal and random universe.

For society at large, God became irrelevant, to the point where a famous late-twentieth-century *Time* magazine cover declared Him dead.

Into a void without God came naturalism, the dominant view in our culture today.

Widely known author and lecturer Charles Colson, who magnificently applies rational thought to the validity of a Christian worldview in his book *How Now Shall We Live?* expresses it this way:

> Naturalism begins with the fundamental assumption that the forces of nature alone are adequate to explain everything that exists...naturalists say that in the beginning were the particles, along with blind, purposeless natural laws. That nature created the universe out of nothing, through a quantum fluctuation. That nature formed our planet, with its unique ability to support life. That nature drew together the chemicals that formed the first living cell. And naturalism says that nature acted through Darwinian mechanisms to evolve complex life-forms and, finally, human beings, with the marvels of consciousness and intelligence.

Without God in nature, then, against the vastness of an impersonal universe, man has no more or less meaning than a rock or a tree.

And so Hobbes replies to Calvin.

"It kind of makes you wonder why man considers himself such a screaming big deal."

The acceleration of accumulated knowledge that began with the cultural paradigm shift of the Renaissance is staggering.

For the first 10,000 years of recorded human history, the fastest that any human could travel was the speed of a galloping horse—unless someone wanted to jump off a building or a cliff.

It's only in the last hundred years or so—the last two or three generations, a tiny blink of time—that technology has allowed us to travel much faster. Some cars go as fast as 200 miles an hour. Airplanes can go faster than sound. A journey that took the early American settlers weeks or months by wagon over dangerous territory, we can accomplish in hours on an interstate in air-conditioned comfort.

In fact, thanks to science and technology, most of us truly live better than kings did only 100 years ago. We live in heated homes with running water, televisions, and washers and dryers. Doctors no longer try to cure us by applying leeches to parts of our body to suck blood; we can get the best of modern drugs and operations. We're protected by electronic security systems and police forces; we probably don't lie awake at night worrying about barbarians tearing down our town. We store our wealth in electronic binary codes in bank computers, not in piles of gold or silver that armies can steal.

And these improvements in science and technology are happening faster and faster. A little more than 30 years ago, man first stepped on the moon; now sport-utility vehicles have more technology than the first spaceships, and your desktop computer has more calculating power than the computers that placed the first men on the moon. With cell phones and computers, you can instantly communicate through satellites to locations anywhere in the world.

Medicine? Your body can be vaccinated, wired, and cloned.

Even color televisions were first invented only 40 years ago. Now you can entertain yourself with the virtual reality of music videos, computer games, and theater screens three stories tall.[3]

With this rush of knowledge, we've conquered nature by insulating ourselves against it and, except for a few loose ends, by believing we understand it.

The only relevance nature has in our daily lives is what's happening on the weather channel.

"That's why we stay inside with our appliances."

The paradox is that as we smugly insulate ourselves so thoroughly from the natural world and focus on becoming the center of our tiny universes, a cynical disbelief in the existence of God denies us from possibly making that claim.

In 1935, influential scientist—and outspoken atheist—Bertrand Russell summed the attitude of twentieth-century intellectuals with this statement in his classic book *Religion and Science:* "Before the Copernican revolution, it was natural to suppose that God's purposes were specifically concerned with the earth, but now this has become an unplausible hypothesis."

Everything in science to that point suggested his conclusion about the data was inarguable. At the subatomic level, classic nuclear physics had explained the mysteries of the atom, and quantum physics was taking it a step further. At the cosmic level, Einstein's theory of relativity was expanding Newton's mechanical explanation of the workings of the universe. And on a planetary level, Darwin had explained the existence and development of life.

Some even declared that science had neared the end of its journey. What more was there to know?

This was 1935.

In the next decades, quantum physics succeeded in replacing much of the cherished truths of classic nuclear physics, and in bringing new mysteries. Atoms were particles and waves at the same time; matter could flicker in and out of existence.

Experimental work on Einstein's theories brought as many questions as it answered.

And mainstream biologists began to see that patterns in the fossil record did not match the predictions of Darwin.

Then came the staggering proof that the universe had a beginning. With universal acceptance of the big bang theory and a universe with a definite starting point, the Genesis view of a created universe suddenly had substance.

Science, astoundingly, was opening the door to the existence of God again.

Yet naturalism prevails in popular culture.

Why?

The first to blame is the media. (Which usually gets the blame for most of our evils. And despite this, becomes more pervasive each year.)

Conflict sells. Harmony doesn't.

The fringes of both science and religion get the most press.

Result?

What we see are extreme fundamentalists disagreeing with out-of-the-box science in news clips of 30 seconds or less.

So popular culture finds it difficult to understand good faith or good science.

Or the reconciliation of both.

A much more mundane target, I believe, should shoulder much more of the blame than the media:

High school science.

For most of us, the extent of our scientific knowledge ends in high school, where it is unlikely that we cared or

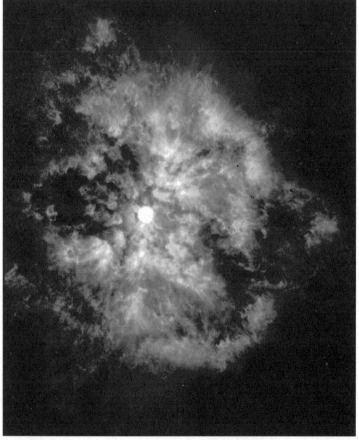

Yves Grosdidier, Anthony Moffat, Giles Joncas, Agnes Acker, and NASA

Hubble telescope picture of energetic star WR 124 surrounded by hot clumps of gas being ejected into space at speeds of over 100,000 miles per hour

understood much anyway. (Face it, you had much better things to do at that time of your life.)

Worse, as a generalization with great validity, high school science is science frozen in time, decades behind the latest in science.

While the teachers aren't necessarily to blame, there is an obvious point to be made. If they were scientists, aware of the new frontiers, they would not be teaching at a high school level.

Exceptional high school science teachers with a passion for scientific knowledge beyond what is required by curriculum are still handcuffed by the curriculum they have no choice but to teach.

Our accumulation of knowledge is so rapid that if a textbook strove to be current, it would be out of date as the ink on its pages dried. That's presuming that those who set the curriculum are even concerned with radically changing the system and textbooks to bring new science to the classrooms. That would be based on a further presumption that students would be given time to learn classic nineteenth- and twentieth-century science as a foundation to understanding new science and the questions which arise from it.

And all of this would be based on the presumption that questions of God arising from new science would be allowed back into the classrooms of public schools.

The end result is that high school science doesn't give much more than an understanding of classic nuclear physics, Newton's mechanical view of the universe, and Darwin's theory of evolution.

In other words, most high school graduates today are hampered by the same scientific limitations that Bertrand Russell faced in 1935 when he declared God's purpose with Earth as an "unplausible hypothesis."

Yet since then, another few generations of science have brought astounding evidence of a created universe.

Science, unlike Bertrand Russell, is no enemy of God.

The temptation for intellectuals is to feel amused sympathy for the church leaders who wrongly used the Bible to make scientific judgments that subsequent data and experimentation easily proved wrong.

As scientific discoveries show more and more the face of God, perhaps within another half century intellectuals will reserve that same amused sympathy for atheist Bertrand Russell and the pitiful lack of knowledge that brought him to his own misguided conclusion.

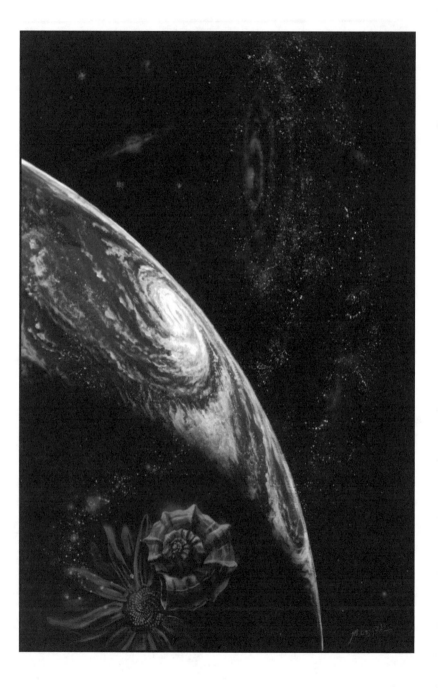

5

The Anthropic Principle

An explosion in a junkyard does not lead to sundry bits of metal being assembled into a useful working machine.[4]

ASTRONOMER FRED HOYLE,
who coined the phrase "big bang"

Anyone equipped with only high school science is at the least decades behind, and often, with the theory of evolution, over a century behind the frontier today. Because of this, little in public school science will point students toward the existence of God.

Yet the following scientific knowledge, for example, has been available for four decades:

In the 1960s, physicists began to notice an extraordinary common denominator among coincidences in the laws of physics that could not be explained in any other rational way: *All of these mysterious values and relationships in physics had been necessary for the creation of life.*

Fast forward to the next decade, to the fall of 1973, to a gathering of the world's best astronomers and physicists as they commemorated the five-hundredth birthday of the father of modern astronomy, Nicolaus Copernicus.

Here, a well-respected astrophysicist and cosmologist from Cambridge University, Brandon Carter, presented a paper with a ponderous title: "Large Number Coincidences and the Anthropic Principle in Cosmology."

The contents of his paper were anything but ponderous.

Based on science that had been charted since Bertrand Russell's *Religion and Science*, Carter argued what some astronomers and physicists had been beginning to wonder since the 1960s. He called it the anthropic principle, from the Greek word for man, *anthropos*.

At the beginning of this book, I made the point that there is a vast difference between inarguable data and arguable conclusion. Carter's thinking is a good example of it. He gathered all the inarguable scientific data that related to the constants in physics—gravity, weak nuclear forces, strong nuclear forces, electromagnetism—that were necessary for the creation of life. Then he drew the conclusion that many in science were trying to avoid.

Perhaps, Carter said, there was no coincidence to the number of strange and seemingly random coincidences that led to the existence of the universe and to the existence of life.

Perhaps all of it had been arranged around the central task of producing humankind.

To appreciate what this meant, I needed a crash course in physics. I needed to see a picture in my head of the physics constants at work. Gravity? Weak nuclear forces? Strong nuclear forces? Electromagnetism?

I learned that all four of the fundamental forces in physics interact on an atomic level, which has profound consequences on a cosmic level.

Quantum physics will give us a picture of the atom, although in fact it's much more complicated than what I'm about to present and must be truly understood through mathematical equations. (Which it why I prefer to rely on pictures!)

An atom contains at its core a nucleus of protons and neutrons bound together by the strongest force in the universe, the strong nuclear force. Electrons buzz in orbit around the nucleus, held to the core by the weak nuclear force.

Although it's not quite accurate, think of it as a mini–solar system. The nucleus is the sun, and the electrons are planets circling the sun. The main difference is that electrons don't circle in predictable linear orbits; they buzz at such an incomprehensible rate it is impossible to predict or map their movement.

Atoms are so small that the smallest speck that can be seen under a microscope is wide enough to contain 10 billion atoms. Yet if the nucleus of one hydrogen atom were the size of a tennis ball, the orbit of the single electron around it would be a sphere of four miles. Four miles!

While that might seem like a lot of space between the single electron and the nucleus, this electron moves so quickly it has the effect of a fan blade moving with the power of a jet turbine. When the blades are motionless, you could easily put a finger in the space between the blades, but at full speed, the blades are essentially taking up all the space and your finger would...well, you get the picture. The entire atom—consisting of its nucleus and an orbiting electron—is effectively, then, a cohesive and almost impenetrable sphere.

Complex as this seems, hydrogen—element one, with one proton and one electron—is the simplest element in the universe. An element such as uranium 238 has 146 neutrons and 92 protons at its core, with dozens and dozens of electrons at various levels of orbit, buzzing each of their spheres of orbit at a fantastic speed that makes jet turbines look like they're rotating at a snail's pace.

Every atom and every molecule in the entire universe contain this incredible, complicated dance of proton, neutron, electron, and all the other subatomic particles. The dance is played to an equally complicated symphony of music that is the perfect interaction of gravity, electromagnetism, and strong and weak nuclear forces.

The consistency of this is predictable and unchangeable, as given by the physics constants that science has charted.

This complicated interaction of all four forces is mind-boggling enough. Then consider what happens if any of those physics constants are altered in the slightest.

Everything in the universe—literally—falls apart.

Roughly 30 years ago, after the big bang theory had been widely established—more on the big bang next chapter—physicists ran computer programs that literally let them play God. By then, enough data had been assembled to allow them to understand the beginning moments of the universe. They began to try to theoretically recreate the universe by tinkering with those four fundamental forces of physics—gravity, electromagnetism, the strong nuclear force, and the weak nuclear force.

These physicists "evolved" hypothetical universes where the force of gravity was a few percentage points less. Then more. Where electromagnetism—the relationship between electricity and magnetism, which is fundamentally important to the electrical attraction in an atom's orbit—was strengthened or weakened. Where the strong nuclear force—the bond between protons and neutrons at the core of an atom's nucleus—was infinitesimally altered. Where they played with the weak nuclear force—the interaction between electrons and the nucleus of an atom.

They discovered easily and quickly that the slightest changes in any of the four fundamental forces would result in a universe totally devoid of life.

So far, this may not seem impressive in an argument for the anthropic principle.

Think of it this way.

You *could* win a state lottery this week. It's not likely, but if you did, it wouldn't seem unbelievable. Someone, after all, has to win.

In terms of what is needed for a universe that produces life, call the probability of winning this week's lottery, as a rough example, the probability that gravity is just the right proportion in comparative weakness to the force of electromagnetism.

To be exact, data shows that gravity is about 10^{39} times weaker.

Here, I'd like to pause for a moment. While you probably know that 10^{39} is a short form of notation for a ten followed by 39 zeroes, I think it's important to look at the actual number: 10,000,000,000,000,000,000,000,000,000, 000,000,000,000.

Gravity, the weakest known force in the universe, is this many times weaker than the force of electromagnetism.

Yet if gravity were only 10^{33} times weaker—10,000,000, 000,000,000,000,000,000,000,000,000 instead of 10,000, 000,000,000,000,000,000,000,000,000,000,000,000—the mass of stars would be a billion times less massive, and as a result, would burn a million times faster.

Life would not exist.

That's just one physics constant absolutely necessary for the creation of life.

Could you win the same lottery for the second week in a row? Certainly it's possible. Unlikely as it might be, "probability" means that you can't eliminate "never."

If the right constant of gravity is like winning the lottery in week one, then winning week two is like discovering that the nuclear weak force is exactly correct in comparison to the force of gravity to enable a universe that sustains life.

Keep in mind that gravity is 10^{39} times weaker than electromagnetism. At the same time, for the universe to have life, the nuclear weak force must be 10^{28} times stronger than gravity. In mathematics, this 10^{28} notation is used for simplicity, but the same simplicity, unless you think about it carefully, reduces the sheer magnitude of what's involved. Tedious as it might seem to once again show all the zeroes, I think it's important to try to comprehend the almost incomprehensible, so here's the translation:

The force that keeps an electron attached to the nucleus of an atom is 100,000,000,000,000,000,000,000,000, 000,000 times stronger than the opposing pull of the force of gravity.

If the weak nuclear force were just slightly less than 10^{28} times stronger than gravity, the attraction between the single electron and the single proton at the core of hydrogen would be distorted just enough that all hydrogen in the universe would have turned into helium, with its two protons and two electrons.

No hydrogen, no water. No water, no life.

Imagine the headlines after you'd won three state lotteries in three consecutive weeks.

That's like the mathematical chance that, along with the relationship between gravity and electromagnetism, and the relationship between gravity and the weak nuclear force, the strong nuclear force is just exactly right to create this universe as it exists.

But reduce the strong nuclear force by as little as two percent, and protons would not exist at the nuclear core, thus producing a universe without atoms.

Reducing it by five percent means a universe without stars.

With that force exactly right to sustain this universe as it is, you've just won the lottery again.

But you haven't finished your monopoly on winning each week's state lottery. Number four in a row is like discovering that if the difference in mass between a proton and neutron were not exactly as is, neither would be distinguishable from the other.

Chemistry would not exist, therefore life would not exist.

And here you are, the winner of the fifth consecutive state lottery, with the fact that carbon is able to exist. How important is carbon? It's the key element capable of fusing the long, molecular chains of protein, fat, and all compounds needed for life, including DNA.

Yet, except for an astounding coincidence, carbon should not be able to be formed.

Here's the physics: Carbon is number six in the periodic table of elements, with hydrogen (1), helium (2), lithium (3), beryllium (4), and boron (5) coming before it.

The math of the formation of carbon is simple. Take the nucleus of helium—two protons, two neutrons—and combine it with the four protons and four neutrons at the core of beryllium. The end result is the six protons and six neutrons in the carbon nucleus.

What makes the formation of carbon possible is the ratio of the strong nuclear force to the constant of electromagnetism. Any variation in this ratio, and it would be impossible for the binding of helium and beryllium to take place at the temperature typical of the center of a star. Because to make this possible, beryllium must be energized to an excited state where it is unstable enough to interact with another element.

The life span of this excited state is 10^{-17} seconds. In other words, a helium nucleus has .00000000000000001 seconds to find, collide, and be absorbed by a beryllium nucleus. And at this excited state, it has to match perfectly with the ratio of the strong nuclear force to electromagnetism, a coincidence scientists call "astonishing."

Nitrogen, oxygen, and the other heavy elements required for life are built on the nuclear reactions that follow the formation of carbon. Without carbon as a bridge, the universe would consist almost exclusively of hydrogen and helium. Everything, then, depends on matching the energies of hydrogen, the unstable beryllium, and the formation of carbon. And by the way, with all the forces that must be perfectly matched at the perfectly right temperature for the production of carbon, this foundation of life is the fourth most abundant element in the universe.

Random coincidence?[5]

Famous astronomer Fred Hoyle admitted that his atheism was greatly shaken when he calculated the chances of this happening by accident. He wrote this in the November 1981 issue of *Engineering and Science:*

A common sense interpretation of the facts suggests that a superintellect has monkeyed with physics, as well as with chemistry and biology, and that there are no blind forces worth speaking about in nature. The numbers one calculates from the facts seem to me so overwhelming as to put this conclusion beyond question.

The list continues. At a cosmic level, the ratio between the initial velocity of the big bang—the explosion that began the universe from a point of nothingness—and the force of gravity was perfect for the formation of the universe. Had gravity been stronger or the velocity less, the universe would have collapsed upon itself. Too much velocity or too little gravity, and all matter would have expanded too quickly for the stars and galaxies to form.

How fine was this difference? Accurate to within one part in 10^{60}. Yes, ten followed by 60 zeroes! One British physicist, Paul Davies, writes, "such stunning accuracy is surely one of the great mysteries of cosmology."

Here's the world's most recognized cosmologist, Stephen Hawking, commenting on the same issue:

Why did the universe start out with so nearly the critical rate of expansion that separates models that recollapse from those that go on expanding forever, so that even now...it is still expanding at the critical rate? If the rate of expansion one second after the big bang had been smaller by even one part in a hundred thousand million, the universe would have recollapsed before it ever reached its present state.

Indeed, why?

Want mystery and "coincidence" at the beginning of creation?

Astronomer Fred Hoyle wrote this (emphasis mine):

> ...even in its supposedly first second [of existence] the universe...*has to know in advance what it is going to be before it knows how to start itself.* For in accordance to the Big Bang Theory, for instance, at a time of 10^{-43} seconds, the universe has to know how many types of neutrino [a subatomic particle that has no electric charge] there are going to be at the time of 1 second. This is so in order that it starts off expanding at the right rate to fit the eventual number of neutrino types.

This is what it takes, then, to believe the universe was not created: Without even addressing why or how the universe suddenly sprang into being, you need to accept the fact that the universe *had to somehow know ahead of time* how it was going to evolve.

And that it had to fine-tune these exact physics constants all in relationship to the others. That's just to create a universe that would successfully remain in existence.

The set of circumstances are even more incredible for our planet to exist as a tiny and fragile life-containing bubble floating in the cosmic extremes of the rest of the universe.

Clementine spacecraft images of the Earth and the moon

Scientists estimate that the probability of the creation of the proper atmosphere with the coinciding establishment of the water cycle during the creation of Earth is one in a hundred trillion trillion (one in 10^{26}).

How distinctive and unlikely does this factor alone make the existence of life on Earth?

Among the hundred billion stars in our galaxy, and the hundred billion other galaxies—multiply those two numbers by each other!—a generous estimate of other existing planets has been pegged at 10^{22}.

A one in 10^{26} chance to get the right combination of atmosphere and water means if there were 10^{26} planets, only one would have that combination. But if there are only 10^{22} planets, the likelihood that this occurrence was random is reduced by a factor of 10,000....

Forget all the other "coincidences" needed for life on Earth. We hit the lottery big-time just to be able to have atmosphere and water.

But there's more needed for life to exist here.

Our planet's orbit is at exactly the right distance from the sun. Two to five percent closer, too hot. Two to five percent farther away, too cold. Most planets in our solar system have elliptical orbits that vary that much in either direction.

If Earth had the same elliptical type of orbit, even at an

Courtesy U.S. Geological Survey/JPL

Clementine spacecraft images of the Earth and the moon

Courtesy U.S. Geological Survey/JPL

Clementine spacecraft image of the Earth

average of the perfect 93 million miles from the sun, each year our planetary temperatures would plunge and rise at variations that would extinguish life.

Yet our planet's orbit is the exception. Nearly a perfect circle.

And the tilt of our planet to the sun is exactly the right angle to foster life.

Coddled at the exact perfect distance from our energy source, we live on a planet with a temperature variation that is negligible compared to temperatures in the rest of the universe that vary from absolute zero to millions of degrees.

Life here depends not only on a hospitable landscape produced by this extremely narrow and unlikely temperature range, but on chemical reactions that can only happen within the shield that Earth's atmosphere gives us.

It's a bubble so cosmically minute that it is almost frightening to consider.

The universe extends for billions of light years in every direction. (A light year is the distance that light will travel at the speed of 186,000 miles per second.)

Yet it only takes 60 miles to exit the bubble of life-giving atmosphere that protects us from the frigidness of that infinite vacuum around us.

A slower or faster rotation of the Earth eliminates life.

A smaller or larger Earth eliminates life.

A smaller or larger moon eliminates life.

A thinner or thicker crust eliminates life.

A lesser or greater ratio of oxygen to nitrogen eliminates life.

A lesser or greater amount of ozone eliminates life.

Also to be noted, of course, are the unique properties of water, the only known substance with a solid phase less dense than the liquid phase. If ice didn't float, no marine life.

But the microscopic properties of water are the truly amazing ones, allowing it to shape proteins and nucleic acids in DNA.

Water, the one substance most needed for life, is also the most abundant substance on our planet.

Could you win the lottery ten weeks in a row? Twenty weeks in a row? Every week for a year?

Say the odds of winning once are one in 10^7, one in ten million. Then the odds of winning twice in a row are one in 10^{14}, one in a hundred thousand billion.

Mathematicians say that if the probability is less than one in 10^{50}, it is essentially impossible or beyond reason. Like, for example, someone picking the correct lottery numbers seven times in a row. At that point, a mathematician would declare the lottery rigged. In essence, it would no longer be a lottery, but something that happens by design.

The essential argument of the anthropic principle is based on this. The mathematical probability that the staggering amount of "astonishing" physics coincidences it takes for the universe to exist in a way that makes life possible cannot be reasonably expected to be accounted for by randomness.

In effect, from a scientific point of view, the supporters of the anthropic principle tell us that humanity is apparently the end goal of the universe.

Here's another way of thinking about it.

You could go for a hike in the mountains and by chance see a rock that, viewed from exactly the right angle, looks like a giant nose. Later, perhaps, you could imagine an ear in the shape of another overhanging boulder. A chin somewhere else. And so on.

We would agree that these are coincidences—random chances that wind and water had happened to shape certain rocks certain ways.

But if you saw all the parts carved perfectly no matter what angle you viewed it, then saw all the parts assembled perfectly to form a giant human face on the side of a mountain—like at Mount Rushmore—you would never believe chance had managed to shape it.

You would declare that it had been designed.

Strongly as all these "coincidences" argue the element of design, there is much more that makes non-deist physicists and astronomers squirm as they try to fit science into a universe without God.

It's called the big bang.

6
No Beginning, No God?

The big bang…"is the one place in the universe where there is room, even for the most hard-nosed materialist, to admit God."

British physicist Paul Davies

Our universe had a beginning!

This might not be news to readers of Genesis, but to the science world in the second half of the twentieth century, this was staggering.

The scientific evidence for the big bang, and how the theory unfolded and eventually became so widely accepted, is almost as fascinating as contemplating the big bang itself.

We truly can peer into the universe and into the beginning of time. We truly can see God's handwriting in the stars.

But first, why atheists in science squirm at the implications of the big bang.

Because, as Charles Colson points out, "Far from supporting naturalism, big bang theory shows the *limits* of all naturalist accounts by revealing that nature itself—time, space, and matter—came into existence a finite period of time ago."[6]

For the last few centuries, as modern science presented the view that the universe was eternal, God was out of the picture.

Accordingly, the Genesis account, with moments of a first creation, was laughable and, within science, ridiculously dogmatic. Believing in God was tantamount to disbelieving the intellectual assertions of science, which had explanations for everything.

In his book *Stephen Hawking's Universe, The Cosmos Explained*, David Filken, a former head of BBC's Television Science department, reflects this attitude:

> For atheistic scientists who wanted to reject the idea of a universe created by God, it was vital to explain how all the known elements had naturally evolved in this universe. It seemed the most effective way to counter the arguments of the religious creationists.

Indeed, without God in the universe, the foundation of naturalist science is that the evolution of the universe and the evolution of life have resulted from endless and purposeless cause and effect. And more importantly, that every step of the cause and effect has an explanation, whether it has been found yet or not.

An eternal universe had fit nicely into this philosophy. No beginning, no God.

Then scientists understood enough to be able to trace cause and effect further and further backward in time.

And the theory of an eternal universe began to crumble, much to their dismay. By the 1960s enough evidence had begun to accumulate that it was more and more difficult to deny that the universe indeed had a beginning.

Not only that, but it was a spectacular beginning—the first cause of all the "cause and effect" events since—with events beyond comprehension.

And with events beyond the explanation of science.

Before the evidence was too strong to ignore, the big bang theory ran into much resistance in the scientific world. The "steady state" universe was the theory through most of the first half of the twentieth century.

It was not so much the evidence that was resisted, but rather the conclusions that had to be drawn from it.

At least one great physicist was honest enough to acknowledge this. Famous in scientific circles, Arthur Eddington called the big bang theory philosophically "repugnant."

Note that.

Philosophy in science.

A determined predisposition to resist the idea of God.

Isn't good science supposed to objectively weigh the evidence first, then come to a conclusion?

The most troublesome issue, then, to those in science "who wanted to reject the idea of a universe created by God" was to discover that once they had traced and explained every step as far back in time as possible, they finally came to this beginning point *totally outside of any scientific explanation.*

In short, this beginning point was an absolute barrier to "seeing" anything that might have happened before.

More frightening were the other questions raised. Why did this "first cause" happen? How was it caused?

More frightening than these questions was the fact that there is no way within science to ever answer these questions.

Let me put it this way. One of the most comforting things in science to a naturalist/non-deist is knowing how all the laws of science work, knowing the predictability, knowing the unchanging permanence of it all. For example, the forces of physics—gravity, the weak nuclear force, the strong nuclear force, and electromagnetism—are universal and eternal. We don't know why those constants are the way they are, but we understand them.

Except.

As science traced events backward to the first fractions of a second of the beginning of the universe, it discovered something equally or more startling and frightening—at least to a determined atheist—than the questions of why and how:

For an almost infinitely small portion of time, as "something" triggered time and this universe to first come

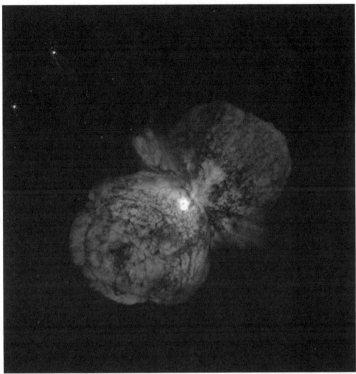

This massive stellar explosion is a mere shadow of the initial cataclysmic birth of the universe

into existence, all known laws of physics break down. They simply do not exist.

It is only *after* the universe comes into existence that physics, as we know it, can be applied to our universe.

The beginning is the great unknowable.

How important theologically is the big bang?

In 1981, the Vatican sponsored a major international conference on scientific cosmology. Given the bad rap that has followed the church since it dealt so shabbily with Galileo, it was a shrewd public relations move. It also showed that the church sensed the shift caused by new cosmic evidence, and was back on safe ground when it came to deism in science.

Pope John Paul II took good advantage of this.

He made this statement to the assembly of physicists who represented the finest scientific minds in the world, a statement that they would be hard-pressed to successfully argue against:

> Any scientific hypothesis on the origin of the world, such as that of a primeval atom from which the whole of the physical world derived, leaves open the problem concerning the beginning of the Universe. Science cannot by itself resolve such a question: what is needed is that human knowledge that rises above physics and astrophysics and which is called metaphysics; it needs above all the knowledge that comes from the revelation of God.[7]

Between the lines, Pope John Paul II was also saying something else: All the incredible scientific progress since the embarrassing Galileo affair nearly five centuries earlier had simply brought God and science full circle.

Listening at this same conference was astrophysicist Stephen Hawking, a man that the *Los Angeles Times* claims "may be the smartest person on the planet."

Indirectly, Stephen Hawking had no choice but to agree with Pope John Paul II, as shown by what Hawking later wrote in his *New York Times* best-seller, *A Brief History of Time:*

> So long as the universe had a beginning, we could suppose it had a creator. But if the universe is really completely self-contained, having no boundary or edge, it would have neither beginning nor end: It would simply be. What place then, for a creator?

This shows the immense difficulty that non-deist science has with a definite beginning to the universe. The best in science have no choice but to agree that if the universe had a beginning, then a beginning point makes room for the possibility of God.

Hawking's search since then has been for an alternative to a universe with a finite beginning. (More on his counterarguments in a later chapter.)

There is irony in his efforts, for he played a key part in the unfolding of the big bang theory.

And at this point, God looks very much alive, for the more modern science has discovered about the universe, the more science points toward that finite beginning....

7

The Primeval Atom

If the universe began with a hot Big Bang, then such an explosion would have left a relic. Find me a fossil of this Big Bang.

ASTRONOMER FRED HOYLE
1940s radio broadcast,
arguing for a steady state universe

In the 1940s, Hoyle was on safe ground. Until big bang theory could no longer be reasonably disputed, the theory of the steady state universe—a universe that has existed forever—had been favored by science in one form or another, since Aristotle first proclaimed that something could not be created from nothing. As such, the steady state universe stood in direct opposition to any account that told us God was responsible for creation.

But if Hoyle had intended to mock the concept of a universe with a beginning, he failed in a way that perhaps God intended with some humor. For the name he derisively coined for the theory during that radio broadcast is how it has been remembered since its validation. More ironic, Hoyle's challenge to find the fossil of the big bang theory actually led to some of its final proofs.

Now?

The big bang vindicates the Genesis account as an uncanny and eerily wonderful description of the incomprehensible. For Genesis, like cosmology, tells us that the universe did indeed burst forth from "nothing."

Perhaps the best way to understand science's explanation of the creation of the universe is to learn how the big bang theory unfolded, a story almost as fascinating as the science that makes it so difficult to dispute. It involves a group of Dutch musicians on a train, a boxer turned lawyer turned astronomer, a genius named Einstein, an obscure Jesuit priest who dared to publicly disagree with him, Hoyle's radio challenge, and much later, two Bell Laboratory researchers who wondered if pigeon droppings interfered with the satellite reception of their gigantic horn antenna.

First:

As you probably remember from basic high school physics, light travels at 186,000 miles per second. (This speed applies in a vacuum. Mind boggling as it seems, in different mediums, physicists are able to literally slow light down to the speed of a baby's crawl.)

Fast as light travels, like sound it still has a finite speed. In a sense, then, we live in a permanent time warp, seeing and hearing events only as they have happened in the past.

Think of observing a lightning strike on the horizon. You see the lightning bolt almost instantly. Almost. If the lightning is a mile a way, it takes $1/186,000^{th}$ of a second for the light to reach your eyes. Because the delay is so minute, for all practical purposes, you saw the strike as it happened. In truth, however, you see an event that has occurred $1/186,000^{th}$ of a second in the past.

Because the speed of light vastly outstrips the speed of sound, this concept is more apparent from the delay between seeing the lightning strike and hearing the thunder that rolls from it. For when the thunder of a lightning bolt reaches your ears, that strike a mile away is about seven seconds in the past.

The distances that light and sound must travel to reach our senses, then, affect how far in the past we can see and hear an event. On Earth, with the relatively short distances involved, this delay is only fractions of milliseconds when it involves the transmission of light waves. In cosmic terms, however, the vast distances that light must travel through the universe to reach Earth make the delay much more significant.

If the sun in our solar system suddenly went dark, for example, we would not know for the period of minutes, the time it takes light to travel 93 million miles. But those minutes are nothing compared to the countless centuries that the light of most of the stars has traveled to reach Earth.

On February 23, 1987, a night assistant at the Las Campanas Observatory in Chile happened to step outside for a break and saw a bright star he'd never noticed before.

There was a good reason for this. Until that night, the star had been a lot dimmer. It was suddenly brighter because it had exploded into a supernova. But not that night.

From the moment that star had burst with the power of millions of hydrogen bombs, the light from the explosion had been steadily traveling toward Earth as our ice ages came and went, as our civilizations rose and fell, as our technology progressed from Stone Age tools to bronze and iron weapons to steam engines to the space ship that carried the first men to the moon.

And then, finally, after traveling at 186,000 miles per second for 160,000 years, light as the messenger of this event reached us here on Earth; when the distance and brightness of this "new" star was confirmed, it turned out to be the first supernova observed since the invention of the telescope.

What other grand cosmic events have occurred hundreds of thousands or even millions of years earlier in different corners of the universe? We may find out any second of any night. We just simply have to wait for the light to arrive, long after the event itself has become ancient history.

What all this means is that the farther away from Earth we can observe with our telescopes, the further we can look back into time.

Generation by generation, science has continued to push the curtains of time farther and farther apart, developing telescope technology that now lets us look into layer after layer of time; the history of the universe has been unscrolled further and further into its past. Astronomers are now able to successively compare what galaxies were like in the near past to much earlier times in the history of the universe, as much as ten billion years back in time. They can literally see how the universe has evolved, looking far enough back that for atheist scientists who would prefer the comfort of an infinite universe, it is almost impossible to deny the beginning of the universe and all that it implies about creation.

The light that reaches us shows the handwriting of God across the universe. And the first scientist to begin to decipher it was Christian Doppler, who discovered the principle named after him in 1842 in Vienna.

Nearly 30 years before, while heating different elements, a German lens manufacturer named Joseph von Fraunhofer had noticed predictable variations in the patterns of lines in the spectrum of refracted light from those chemicals.

Doppler used this to go a step further, showing that the speed of a star could be determined by measuring the apparent change in the frequency of its light waves.

This, in the unfolding story of the big bang, is where the Dutch musicians make their appearance.

The most famous experiment to confirm the Doppler effect took place in a train station in Holland, conducted—pardon the pun—by Christopher Buys-Ballot, who put that group of musicians on a train and asked them to play a constant note. As the train rushed first toward him and then away from him without stopping at the platform, Buys-Ballot was able to detect the distinct change in pitch of that note. Listeners on the train, however, heard only the one steady note.

The explanation is fairly simple.

As the train gets closer, it takes progressively less time for the sound to reach the listener. The waves of sound become "squashed" on the approach, resulting in a higher pitch. The opposite happens as the train recedes; the lengthening gap between the observer and the source means the sound waves are effectively "stretched," so that the observer hears a lower pitch. Meanwhile, those on the train remain a constant distance from the sound, so they hear a constant pitch.

This "squashing and stretching" is called the Doppler effect.

While it is much more difficult from everyday experience to understand this same principle with light, once again, the vast distances of the universe prove to be significant for observers on Earth.

Light, like sound, travels in waves. (And as particles, but that's another discussion.) Unlike sound, the difference in the "squashing" or "stretching" of light waves does not result in a different pitch. What does change, however, are parts of the light spectrum. Visible light, as demonstrated by refraction through a prism, breaks down into the colors of a rainbow. Shorter waves are at the top or blue end. Longer waves at the bottom, or red.

Christian Doppler decided that the wavelengths of the light from stars could tell him whether they were approaching or receding from Earth. It turned out to be a very accurate guess. By refracting the starlight of different stars at different points in their orbits, he observed red shifts as they receded and blue shifts as they approached.

Since then, for example, the changing red and blue shifts of two stars of Alpha Centauri have been studied long enough to show that they complete their orbits around each other every 80 years.

For astronomers of the nineteenth century, the Doppler effect was simply a useful tool to confirm what they expected from the orbits they had already observed: the universe contains movement of individual stars and other heavenly bodies.

But for another seven decades no one thought to wonder about the movement of the universe itself.

And when that person did, what he learned staggered the scientific world.

Edwin Hubble.

Hubble was good enough with his fists to contemplate becoming a boxer, and good enough with his brains to earn a Ph.D. in law at Oxford. Instead of making his fame in a canvas ring or courtroom, however, he found it on a mountaintop in California.

Edwin Hubble's goal in the 1920s was to map the universe galaxy by galaxy. He gained access to the Mount Wilson Observatory in California, which at that time held the most powerful optical telescope in the world.

By using the Doppler effect to study the refraction of starlight, Hubble identified the elements in the stars and also the direction and speed of the galaxies. He and his team confirmed, with no sense of surprise, that analysis of light spectrums showed hydrogen and helium to be the most abundant elements in those galaxies.

They did notice something else that was extremely peculiar and difficult, at first, for them and other scientists to comprehend or believe.

And around that time, halfway across the world, a persistent Jesuit priest was trying to convince Albert Einstein to admit to the "biggest blunder" of his life.

By then, early in the twentieth century, the scientific world had placed Einstein on a demigod level.

For good reason.

Isaac Newton's laws of physics predicted how most of the universe functioned, but constant observational tests showed slight and nagging imperfections, like the orbit of the planet Mercury, which had an unseemly wobble.

Until Einstein, science had to live with the imperfections of a Newtonian universe. But Einstein's genius allowed him to understand that gravity and light and time don't behave on cosmic levels the way they do in our everyday commonsense lives.

While Newton described gravity as the relational attraction between two objects of different size—hence the famous apple falling to the ground—Einstein revised it completely, hypothesizing that gravitational effects are a consequence of the fact that cosmic objects affect a grid of space and time. Gravity affects the space around it. Furthermore, and much more difficult to comprehend from daily life observations, gravity affects the speed of time. And can bend light.

The mathematical equations he proposed showed it to be true on a cosmic level.

Essentially, the heavier the object the more of a "dent" it makes in space and time.

Space-time? Dents?

Stretch a thin rubber blanket among four people. Think of that as a grid of space and time.

Place a heavy cannonball in the center. Think of that as a massive star.

The weight of the ball will sink into the rubber, creating a dent, with the ball remaining at the bottom, just the way a massive star bends space and time around it.

Take a marble. This is a planet.

Spin the marble above the cannonball, around the walls of the dent in the rubber sheet. If the marble moves too slowly, it will sink into the dent. If it moves too quickly, it will fly out of the walls of the dent. At just the right speed—think of a racecar moving through a banked corner—the marble will maintain orbit above the cannonball.

This, roughly speaking, was Einstein's concept of space-time, which he defined through those mathematical formulas that, to the amazement of scientists, were proved correct again and again by later observation.

Time and space is relative to the position of the observer.

Yet Einstein's new view of the universe didn't quite solve everything.

Newton had not been able to explain why—if gravity worked as he predicted—all matter in the universe didn't eventually get pulled together into one big lump.

Einstein's mathematical model—unlike Newton's—showed that the universe could not remain motionless. But since Einstein was convinced the universe was eternal and infinite, he theorized that there had to be some factor that allowed local variations without affecting the overall constant and unchanging status of the entire universe. He called it the "cosmological constant," a weakly repulsive force to cancel any inward pull of gravity that would force the universe to eventually collapse. To make his equations work perfectly, Einstein added this arbitrary and extra factor to his equations.

Because of Einstein's stature and the way all his other predictions had proved so uncannily accurate, the scientific world did not dispute him.

Except for that persistent Jesuit priest.

Georges Lemaître.

In the 1920s, Lemaître was the leading theoretical cosmologist at the Vatican Observatory in the high hills south

Michael Rich, Kenneth Mighell, James D. Neill, Wendy Freedman, and NASA

Hubble Telescope view of globular cluster called G1 in a neighboring galaxy

of Rome. If he could find a scientific way to support a finite beginning, then he (and the Catholic Church which supported his research) would finally be able to argue that the creationist ideas in the Bible were consistent with the new knowledge of the nature of the universe.

As Einstein's theories about space-time suggested the universe ought to be gently contracting or expanding, Lemaître studied them with great interest. He knew that Einstein had arbitrarily added the "cosmological constant" to fit the current scientific prejudice that the universe was eternal. This, of course, ruled out a moment of creation.

Lemaître, unafraid to search for or see God behind the universe, simply removed Einstein's arbitrary factor from the equations. Mathematically, this allowed for the expansionary force to counter or exceed the gravitational force everywhere in the universe, leading to the model of a universe that was always expanding.

Lemaître mused further. If the universe was expanding now, that meant it had been smaller in the past. If that were true, then the further back in time, the smaller it would have been. The logical conclusion to this was a point in time, a very, very long time ago, when the universe would have been at its very smallest. The point at which it had been created. The "primeval atom," as Lemaître decided to call it.

This was the scientific model of the universe that Lemaître—and his church—had been seeking. The universe had sprung and grown from that beginning point, like a plant from a seed. Two exciting things about this model seemed to strongly support it: the model followed all the mathematics of Einstein's model, and, better yet, also solved the problems of expansion that Einstein's model predicted.

There was one problem with Lemaître's theoretical model.

Einstein didn't like it. Unimpressed, Einstein even went as far as to ridicule the notion of a primeval atom and a moment of creation. Einstein called Lemaître's grasp of physics poor, and declared it was "obvious" the universe must be eternal, infinite, and unchanging.

Whom would the scientific community believe? Einstein? Or a Jesuit priest with a perceived religious agenda and a bizarre hypothesis?

But unknown to Einstein and Lemaître, in California, Edwin Hubble was patiently mapping the galaxies of the universe.

On Mount Wilson, Hubble's team had discovered that all the spectrums of light they analyzed from distant galaxies were red-shifted. The light waves from those galaxies were longer, telling them that every galaxy in every direction was moving away from ours. More peculiar was the fact that the farther away the galaxy, the more it was red-shifted. In other words, as distance increased, so did the speed. Not only was the universe expanding in all directions, but it was an accelerated expansion!

If this was true, it suggested that atheist scientists could no longer believe in an unchanging and infinite universe, a concept they were reluctant to embrace even when they could not deny the evidence.

For Lemaître, it was news that perhaps he had prayed for, and certainly hoped for—scientific evidence to suggest his model of an expanding universe was far from far-fetched.

But how to convince Einstein, and in so doing, the rest of the scientific community?

As a result of Hubble's work, Einstein wanted to spend time with him for further discussion. When Lemaître learned of this, he arranged to lecture at the California Institute of Technology at the same time Einstein was visiting Hubble.

Lemaître found a chance to speak to them both at the same time. Step by step, he argued the theory of the primeval atom. More importantly, Lemaître painstakingly worked through all the mathematics.

Then Lemaître watched Einstein and Hubble and held his breath.

Einstein, after all, was inarguably the greatest scientist since Newton. The man who had earlier called Lemaître's theory ridiculous.

Einstein stood and made his pronouncement. Lemaître's model of the universe was, Einstein said, "the most beautiful and satisfying interpretation I have listened to." Moreover, Einstein admitted the "cosmological constant" had been the "biggest blunder" of his life.

Those of faith—inside or outside Lemaître's Catholic church—now had a scientifically supported moment of creation.

Einstein was convinced of a beginning to the universe. How significant was this to him as a proof of God's existence? He later wrote of his desire "to know how God created this world. I am not interested in this or that phenomenon, in the spectrum of this or that element. I want to know his thought. The rest are details."

Lemaître's triumph was not without opposition.

Lemaître's model of the universe took the data from Hubble's work and projected it backward, not unlike running a movie film in reverse. He was able to use the current expansion speed, and by knowing how far the galaxies were from Earth and each other at different points in time, it became possible to calculate when all the galaxies had been together, some 15 billion years earlier.

This was not the picture of an eternal universe, but of one exploding from what seemed like nothing.

It was the "seemed like nothing" that was most preposterous to those in science who were committed atheists. They correctly argued that Einstein's mathematics also allowed for a contracting universe. Who could really say for certain that our telescopes brought us a picture of the entire universe? Beyond our vision of an expanding universe, they said, another part of the universe could just as easily be contracting. Our corner of the universe could just be a minor bubble in a giant cauldron of boiling water.

Among these scientists was Fred Hoyle, almost as well-known and well-respected in scientific circles as Einstein. Hoyle's work was revolutionary, too. He'd demonstrated that stars had life cycles of birth and death. It showed that stars could come into being and also disappear, with the implication that different parts of the universe could behave in the same way.

Against the notion of the universe springing into being from something smaller than an atom, on a "day which had no yesterday," Hoyle showed scientifically it was very possible to conceive of an eternal universe with changing internal dynamics.

So Hoyle issued his challenge: "If the universe began with a hot Big Bang, then such an explosion would have left a relic. Find me a fossil of this Big Bang."

And nearly two decades later, two Bell Laboratory researchers wondered if pigeon droppings were the cause of unidentifiable interference with reception on their giant antenna.

Even earlier, however, Hoyle's challenge had been partially met, at least in theory.

In 1948, shortly after Hoyle's challenge, physicists Ralph Alpher and Hans Bethe theorized that if the big bang had occurred, it would have generated quadrillions of degrees of heat. They speculated that this heat would have left an afterglow that should be detectable even after billions of years.

Furthermore, they argued, since the universe had expanded in all directions, this heat should be evenly distributed everywhere. It would be difficult to detect, they said, for their calculations placed it at only a couple degrees above absolute zero.

Yet if this background radiation was found spread across the universe, they said, this would be the "fossil" that Hoyle demanded.

Pigeon droppings?

In 1964, literally just down the road from Princeton University, Bob Wilson and Arno Penzias worked as researchers for Bell Laboratories. In preparation for satellite transmission of broadcasting signals, they needed to clean up the reception on a receiver. They had tried everything, including removing pigeons that were nesting on the giant antenna and scraping away the droppings. Not even that worked. The low-level interference seemed to be everywhere.

Someone suggested they call some radiation experts at Princeton.

At Princeton, this team was in pursuit of proof of the big bang's background radiation as predicted by Alpher and Bethe. They were almost ready to scan for low-level radiation in outer space. They had calibrated their instruments to distinguish this radiation from other, more powerful, radiations. They had added what they called a "cold source" to compare it against the temperature of the radiation they were seeking.

The ideal test setup was almost ready. So they took a lunch break.

During lunch, the phone rang.

Answering it would cost them the Nobel Prize.

Robert Dicke, leader of the Princeton team, listened to the information that came on the phone from Wilson and Penzias at Bell Laboratories.

They'd checked the strange interference against a cold source.

It was three degrees Kelvin—only three degrees above absolute zero.

It was every direction they looked in outer space.

Dicke ended the conversation, hung up the phone, and looked at the rest of his team.

"Well, boys," he said, "we've been scooped."

Later awarded the Nobel Prize for this, the telephone company researchers had accidentally stumbled across what the Princeton academics had been trying to find.

Hoyle's fossil of the big bang.

Lemaître's model of a created universe—expanding outward from a singular point in time and space—was almost complete in scientific terms.

But there was more, and what was about to be discovered about the universe would make science fiction look tame....

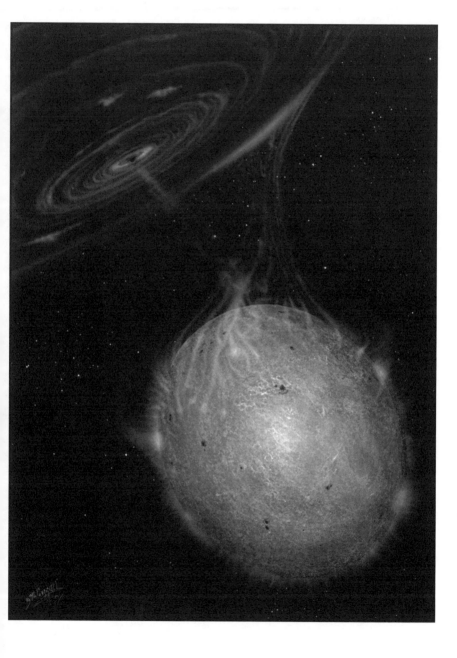

8
Believing the Impossible...

In the beginning God created the heavens and the earth.

GENESIS 1:1

In the beginning, God created the heavens and the earth...from a point with no dimensions?

If so, this truly is "something from nothing"—literally, creation.

This, too, is essentially the "primeval atom" model of the universe proposed by Georges Lemaître in 1927. Backing it up were: observations that confirmed predictions made by Einstein's mathematics of an expanding universe; the "red-shifting" of starlight from Hubble's work that showed our universe expanded in all directions; the "fossil," a barely detectable background radiation of the remnant heat of a "big bang" that permeated the universe.

(By the way, although this background radiation is only 2.73 degrees above absolute zero, because it covers the entire universe, it still contains more energy than all the stars and galaxies, which, hot as they are, are only tiny pinpricks in the area of the whole universe.)

With all this scientific knowledge in the 1960s, there was still some doubt. Theoretically, the universe appeared to be like a rapidly expanding balloon. To explore the beginning of the universe, then, scientists simply took a model of its current expansion and ran it backwards and backwards and backwards. Like sucking the air out of a balloon that had been filling for 15 billion years.

The analogy isn't perfect, and there is one crucial and almost incomprehensible difference.

Filled with air or not, a balloon is the same object; only its shape changes.

On the other hand, running the model of an expanding universe backward—like running a movie backward—made it appear as if all material were collapsing into itself. At the current 15- to 18-billion years of age, all this material fills the area as big as the universe. Far earlier in time, the size of a galaxy. Earlier than that, the size of a star. Fractions of a second after coming into existence, the size of a grapefruit. And before that, an invisible pinpoint. Then, running this model of the universe forward again, it seemed as if the stars and galaxies and cosmic debris suddenly exploded from nothing.

The equivalent with a balloon would be like seeing the rubber appear from nowhere and watching it mushroom outward, then playing a video of it backward and watching it shrink until the rubber disappears completely into thin air.

With a balloon, our everyday and commonsense observations tell us this is so obviously impossible that it is not worth consideration.

All the matter of the universe could be packed into a point of nothingness?

Our own planet has a circumference of 25,000 miles. How could all of it be reduced to a ball the size of a grapefruit, let alone a pinpoint? And then to try to believe the same of all the matter of our solar system and our galaxy and the countless other galaxies of the universe? Not only that, but the most realistic models of the big bang show that in all likelihood the visible matter of this universe comprises only 10 percent—another 90 percent is dark matter, observable only by the gravitational pull it exerts on the movement of galaxies.

All this from an infinitely dense pinpoint that exploded with enough heat to be traced 15 billion years later? (Actually, explosion is not quite accurate. It was a sudden expansion of space that carried matter and energy with it. Think of air suddenly expanding because of a lightning strike, and the heat and noise that blows outward.)

Was the event of the big bang real? Or were all the theories, and the evidence pointing toward those theories, wrong?

One aspect of Einstein's mathematics implied that matter would collapse into a single dense point under the right circumstances, but he refused to believe it could actually happen.

It wasn't until the 1960s that physicists tackled the equations, encouraged by other developments in nuclear physics that let them understand more fully how matter behaved at a subatomic level. They disregarded the "brakes" Einstein had placed upon his own theory, and, with the help of new supercomputers, calculated that if a star was large enough, it would generate such intense gravity as it burned out that all the matter of the star, including its energy, would be drawn into a denser and denser clump of matter until it reached that single dense point as predicted by Einstein. Something this dense would swallow all matter around it, with such gravitational power that not even light would be able to escape.

A black hole.

Going into the 1970s, physicists were finally prepared to accept that this point, termed a "singularity," was real. In theory. But what was needed was evidence that matter could behave this way. For if such a black hole existed, how could it be detected across thousands or millions of light years of space? After all, it would give no light. It would swallow all matter.

And there was another dilemma.

More theoretical work showed that although the collapse of matter was inevitable as predicted by Einstein's equations, it was clear that at the point of "singularity" none of the basic laws of physics would apply.

This was the paradox: the theory said there was a point at which the theory did not work.

Could, then, black holes really exist?

A black hole consists of two things only: a singularity, and an event horizon.

The singularity is the point without dimension where all the mass is contained. It is surrounded by total blackness, for not even light escapes.

The event horizon is the region of space around it that is dark, devoid of light. The larger the mass that is buried in the singularity, the larger the dark area.

At the edges of the event horizon—like being on the edge of a vortex of a giant whirlpool—all matter is driven around so fast by the spin of the black hole that it can be literally hurtled billions of miles into space.

Something with the gravitational pull of a black hole also bends light that gets near the event horizon, but not near enough to be pulled in.

A black hole also exerts a gravitational force on nearby stars, affecting or controlling their orbits.

A black hole close enough to another star strips matter away from the surface of the star and releases huge amounts of X-ray energy.

With all these believed characteristics of a black hole, scientists, then, did not have to see the black hole itself to finally discover it. All they needed to do was rely on an ancient proverb: where there is smoke, there is fire. All they needed to do was find a place where a black hole exerted most or all of its effects on space around it.

By the end of the millennium, they found all the smoke they needed to decide the fire was there.

Cygnus X-1.

The star that cosmologists agree is the first black hole ever discovered.

A point with no dimensions that contains the mass of something thousands of times larger than our sun? How does the impossible become possible?

Ironically, advances at the quantum level in nuclear physics made it possible to understand what happens on a cosmic level.

In comparative terms, the distance between the nucleus of an atom and the circling electrons is huge. (Remember, if the nucleus of one hydrogen atom were the size of a tennis ball, the orbit of the single electron around it would be a sphere of four miles.)

As stars burn out, they no longer create enough energy to generate the pressure that keeps them from collapsing against the force of gravity. A star the size of our sun— 865,000 miles in diameter—will shrink to the diameter of a planet like Earth, only 8,000 miles in diameter. Called a white dwarf, such a star is so dense that one teaspoon of it would weigh several tons here on Earth. (Think of a city bus compressed into the size of a golf ball.)

Yet a neutron star makes a white dwarf look like a puffy snowball. The white dwarf has the mass of our sun reduced to a ball 8,000 miles across; a neutron star consists of the 865,000-mile diameter of our sun compressed into a ball only ten miles across. Here, gravity forces the atoms to be so crammed that the orbiting electrons are squeezed into the protons. The negative charge of the electron is canceled by the positive charge of the proton, and they form neutrons, all tightly packed together.

To give an idea of what this is like, astronomer William A. Gutsch, Jr., has compared the area of a normal atom to an empty Yankee Stadium; its protons and neutrons are like peas on second base, with the electrons

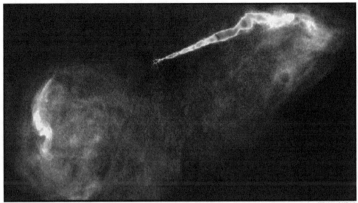

STScI and NRAO

A stream of gas is thrown from a black hole 50 million light-years from Earth

buzzing like gnats above the bleachers. There's a lot of emptiness within the atom.

In a dwarf star, while the atoms are packed tightly side by side, as if a bunch of empty Yankee Stadiums were touching, there is enough space that the electrons can still buzz freely within each empty stadium.

In a neutron star, the atoms are so jammed together, it's as if the buzzing gnats have been forced into the peas, and the once empty side-by-side stadiums are each crammed to the brim with those peas. All the available space is totally filled.

How dense then, is a neutron star compared to a white dwarf? A teaspoon of a neutron star, weighed here on Earth, would be 500 million tons.

In certain situations, however, not even the incredibly dense core of a neutron star will survive against gravity.

When a massive star explodes as a supernova, its core collapses because of intense gravitation forces. If the core—just the core, not the giant star itself—is between 1.4 and three times the size of our sun, gravity collapses that core into the roughly ten-mile wide neutron star.

But a core that is bigger than three times our sun— over 2.5 million miles wide—will not be able to maintain itself against the forces of gravity generated by all that mass. Instead of stopping when the 2.5 million miles of material collapses to a ten-mile wide ball with the density of 500 million tons per teaspoon, the collapse continues, shrinking the core even more. Within a fraction of a second, the core collapses to nothing more than a point with no dimensions. Not even light can escape its gravity.

A black hole.

Why is the existence of black holes so important to the theory of the big bang?

Astrophysicist Stephen Hawking demonstrated to the satisfaction of his peers and to the satisfaction of the laws of physics that the collapse of matter could also be reversed:

If it is possible for something millions of miles across to collapse into a point with no dimensions—as already observed in reality—it is also possible for such an incomprehensible singularity to *expand* from a point with no dimensions, bursting into space and time. And from the next fractions of a second of existence, develop according to the established laws of physics.

This, Hawking proved possible through mathematics, was the big bang.

Here, I would like to repeat the paradox that I mentioned earlier.

At the point of singularity—Lemaître's primeval atom—the laws of physics that make this universe possible do not apply. They do not exist.

Furthermore, nothing in science can speak to the causation of the singularity.

Nor can science answer the reason it exists, the reason it burst into space and time when it did.

Nor how space and time could not exist before each came into being with the big bang.

All this—as any scientist must admit, grudgingly or not—is outside the realm of the natural laws that govern this universe.

As is God.

9

The Foundations
of the Earth

*Where were you when I laid the foundations of
the earth? Tell me, if you know so much. Do
you know how its dimensions were determined
and who did the surveying? What supports its
foundations, and who laid its cornerstone, as
the morning stars sang together and all the
angels shouted for joy?*

GOD SPEAKING TO JOB, JOB 38:4-7

At the beginning of this book, I admitted it has
resulted from a personal search of the findings of science
against what I understood through faith.

To this point, I have represented these findings as well
as I am able, discussing—admittedly in a rough and general way—the overview of how the data of science led to
the conclusion of the big bang theory. (There is much, of
course, that I haven't covered, including the tremendous
work with particle accelerators that has contributed

incredible advances in quantum mechanics and the understanding of the behavior of the nucleus.)

Yet the big bang is still a theory, no matter how
strongly it is supported by quantum physics and cosmology.

This may sound laborious and self-evident, for which I
apologize: You can approach this theory with a certainty
that God exists, and measure what science tells you
against this certainty. Or you can believe God does not
exist, and bleakly try to answer the unanswerable questions raised by the origin of this universe in another way.
Or, from your interpretation of Genesis, you may decide
that after reviewing why science tells us what it does, you
choose to reject either the data of science and/or the implications presented.

I say this simply to explain my own journey. As I tried
to understand the science behind creation, I viewed it from
the foundation that God exists and that, by some means I
can never comprehend in this life, began the process from
outside the realm of all that is natural.

Secure in this faith, it gave me a sense of privilege to be
able to imagine the incredible way God began creation. If
science truly was giving a picture of the beginning of creation—it seemed to me—it was because God was finally
allowing us some of the answers to the questions He had
posed to Job. It took particle accelerators and radio telescopes and satellites and the work of genius after genius
over the course of centuries, but finally, we had a glimpse
of what God had chosen to accomplish....

In the beginning, science acknowledges, there was nothing.

No space. No time.

Then came the awesome moment that space and time were brought into being.

Science can tell us nothing about that moment, for that is the moment within the mind of God. That is the unknowable.

The knowable, within science, occurs 10^{-43} seconds later—this is .oooooooooooooooooooooooooooooooooooooooo ooooooooooo1 seconds—when the entire universe is smaller than a single atom, when the temperature is 10^{33} degrees Fahrenheit, where all of existence is pure energy, not matter. The only force in the universe at this point of birth is gravity. At this temperature, the other future forces of the universe—electromagnetism and the strong and weak nuclear forces—remained coupled to gravity.

Until 10^{-35} seconds after time and space came into being. Now the universe has cooled to 20,000,000,000, 2×10^{27} 000,000,000,000,000,000 degrees Fahrenheit. Cool enough that the strong nuclear force emerges from within the shadows of gravity. Matter doesn't exist in any form yet. Only energy.

10^{-11}

At .oooooooooo1 seconds, the universe has cooled considerably, and is only 20 quadrillion degrees Fahrenheit (20 x 10^{16} degrees). Nature is about to become more complicated. Where there were once only two forces—gravity and the strong nuclear force—now electromagnetism and the weak nuclear force uncouple. The laws of physics—which could not apply in the beginning—are now set.

(These are the same laws with all those amazing "coincidences" that will allow the creation of the universe to unfold as it did in such a way to sustain human life. These are the same laws that the universe had to know ahead of time in order to continue to exist.)

This early in the first moments that time exists, the universe still remains pure energy, a blinding sea of radiation measured in trillions upon trillions of degrees but cooling rapidly as space expands. And finally, at .00001 second, it is cool enough for energy to begin to convert to matter. The first subatomic particles form, particles that will eventually give rise to electrons and protons and neutrons, which will then become atoms.

How much energy does it take to produce matter? The relationship of energy to matter is found in $E=mc^2$, where c^2 is the speed of light multiplied by itself and m is mass. Even a tiny amount of matter, then, contains a huge amount of energy. Conversely, of course, it takes a tremendous amount of pure energy to create a few particles of energy.

Three minutes after time began—when the universe is many trillions of times older than it was in the state of pure energy—its radiation has cooled to a couple of billion degrees. With the values of gravity, electromagnetism, the weak nuclear force, and the strong nuclear force established as they are, protons and neutrons are able to bond to form the first nuclei of atoms. Hydrogen and helium, with one- and two-proton nuclei, respectively, come into existence. As do a small number of nuclei of the next most complex element, lithium, consisting of three protons and three neutrons.

But the universe is cooling so rapidly that within 12 minutes, the fusing process can no longer be sustained. These are the only three elements in the early universe. The other 89 elements will have to wait until billions of years later, when stars and supernovas will generate the heat to forge them.

It will take 300,000 years after the beginning of time for the universe to cool to about 4,000 degrees. Until this point, only the nuclei of hydrogen, helium, and lithium have existed. Not the atoms of these elements. Any electrons that dropped into orbit around the nuclei were immediately ripped away because of the fierce radiation. But at 4,000 degrees the electrons are able to settle into orbit around the nuclei, and the elements are formed.

Something else happens as the electrons join, held in place by the weak nuclear force. Radiation is no longer impeded by the presence of all the free electrons. (Deep within the sun, at temperatures in the millions of degrees, a gamma ray is literally passed from atom to atom and takes several hundred thousand years to escape to the exterior where it becomes visible light. Then, it only takes

NASA

Hubble Telescope view of an active galaxy

about eight minutes to cross the 93 million miles of space to reach Earth.)

At the age of this 300,000 years, the universe is no longer a blinding, seething hotbed of this radiation. The "fog" begins to disappear as the radiation travels outward. Today, this is as far back into time and space that we are able to see. Everything before that is opaque.

After 300,000 years, with the subatomic particles falling into place, gravity begins to clump matter. It is a long process. Finally, as enough hydrogen is massed into the bodies of stars, the gravitational forces ignite nuclear fusion, and stars begin to burn. Then the galaxies of these stars form. And after a billion years, the large-scale structure of the universe is set.

Now come supernovas, stars old enough and big enough to burn themselves into a spectacular collapse at high enough temperatures to form new elements, spewing forth all these elements that will make planets, including our own solar system.

As this material clumps in our own solar system, the Earth is formed in such a way that water and atmosphere will sustain life. Around it, everywhere in space, remains the background radiation, the "fossil" heat of the big bang.

All this came from what was once pure energy, the ignition of space and time brought forth into existence.

Like Job, I can only tremble and wonder in awestruck amazement at how God laid the foundations of the Earth.

10
Atheistic Ideology

The odds against a universe like ours emerging out of something like the big bang are enormous...I think clearly there are religious implications whenever you start to discuss the origins of the universe. There must be religious overtones. But I think most scientists prefer to shy away from the religious side of it.

STEPHEN HAWKING,
to a reporter, following completion
of his work on singularities
and the big bang in 1983

If there is so much evidence to point to a causation of nature that comes from outside of nature—the supernatural—why does the mainstream scientific community apparently resist the notion of God? Why, for example, Arthur Eddington's reaction to early big bang theory and its implications of a Creator as philosophically "repugnant"?

No one, of course, can answer for an individual scientist except for that scientist, so the only guesses I could make are general.

First, is it necessarily true that mainstream science is that resistant? My hunch is that many scientists do, as the quotes in this book show, acknowledge a supernatural Creator, or at least the possibility. Yet to declare a belief in God brings them into philosophical issues far beyond the existence of God, and squarely into the nature of God and the human soul and the purpose of creation, which is outside of science.

Second, evidence may suggest a supernatural Creator, but nothing can—at least within science's present boundaries—empirically prove His existence. Some scientists may find it difficult, as do many outside of science, to take a step of faith. Especially with all the questions that arise in exploration of knowing God. Why is there evil in the world? How has God presented Himself to mankind? Is there an afterlife?

The third reason is one of hubris. If God has created mankind, we are lesser. The notion of not being in ultimate control of human destiny, despite all we are able to do now and in the future through science and technology, is humbling.

Or perhaps Stephen Hawking explained it best when he referred to the "religious" aspect that comes with pursuit of creation. Look back on the shambles of history, and survey—among the shining examples of faith that reflect the love of God—the grief that the man-made distortions of religion have brought upon mankind. It is no wonder when a commonsense scientist tries to avoid religious disputes.

CAN "NOTHING EMPIRICALLY PROVE GOD'S EXISTENCE

Yet all the questions that science raises about the origins of the universe and the orderliness of natural laws do point to a supernatural explanation. And scientists are extremely hard-pressed to come up with an alternative.

For without God, how do you explain from the mathematically impossible "coincidences" in the data behind the anthropic principle, that the laws of physics so perfectly allowed a 15-billion-year process of creating life? How do you explain a universe that had to know in advance how it would develop to survive past the first 10^{-43} seconds of its existence? How do you explain the moment that the universe first burst into time and space from...nothing?

And how do you explain why?

In a naturalistic universe—one that is random and without God—the "why" is explained very simply: because that's the way it is.

The challenge for an atheistic scientist, then, is to prove this is a purposeless naturalistic universe against the scientific evidence that suggests a supernatural Creator.

To do that, it is very important for an atheistic scientist to prove that our universe did not begin at a finite point in time. Stephen Hawking's words bear repeating here:

> So long as the universe had a beginning, we could
> suppose it had a creator. But if the universe is really

purposeless ?
Contradicts all evidence

completely self-contained, having no boundary or edge, it would have neither beginning nor end: It would simply be. What place then, for a creator?

If not a creator, then, how about "parallel" universes as an alternative theory?

Before examining a parallel universe theory, however, here's a quick review of the scientific method.

Early science often depended on reasoning alone. Galileo is often called the father of modern science because he began testing theories with experimental data. (It had been held for centuries that heavier objects fell faster than lighter objects: Galileo proved it wrong after performing carefully designed experiments to study the basic properties of matter in motion. He rolled balls of different weights down inclined planes, discovering that all objects fall to the ground with the same acceleration unless air resistance or some other force slows them down.)

To form a theory or proposed explanation, modern scientists involve some or all of these methods: the observation of nature; classification of data; experimentation; logic; mathematical equations; or computer modeling.

Using these methods, scientific advances come through chance, hard work, or sudden creative insights, but they all have this in common: *A theory will not be accepted as*

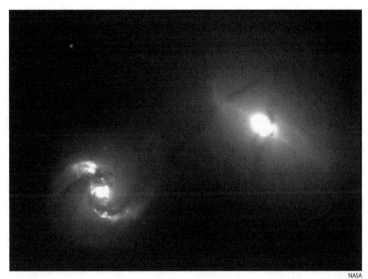

Intergalactic "pipeline" funnels matter between colliding galaxies

scientific knowledge unless other researchers can verify it through repeated experiments.

The big bang theory did involve all these scientific methods. Furthermore, the data can be and has been verified by independent observers. In short, it is solid science at its best, leaving room not for argumentation of the data, but of the conclusion.

So about those parallel universes....

If there are—as the late Carl Sagan said—"billions and billions" of other universes, then from a mathematical and scientific point of view, remote as the possibility is, it *can*

be a random accident that our universe, out of the infinite number of universes, just happened to hit on the right combination of physics constants that produced life. And, of course, our beginning is not really a beginning. Just part of a cycle that involves other universes.

But this supposition clearly steps outside the scientific method. *A theory will not be accepted as scientific knowledge unless other researchers can verify it through repeated experiments.*

This supposition, then, is convenient science fiction speculation, for other universes have neither been observed in practice, nor is it possible to observe them in principle, as, by definition, they are outside our universe.

This theory also ignores the question of the causation of all the other parallel universes.

At one time, famous scientist John Wheeler was the most prestigious proponent of this theory, but he eventually stopped supporting it, saying, "there's too much metaphysical baggage carried along with it...it makes science into some kind of mysticism."

Um, yes.

Alright, if believing in parallel universes takes as much if not more faith than looking for a supernatural Creator, how about turning to "baby" universes as an alternative?

So here is another scientific theory: when a black hole is formed, new baby universes can form with four spacetime dimensions that exist at right angles to the existing one.

Observed in practice?

Observable in principle?
Addresses the causation issue?
Let's move on....

How's this series of premises by another scientist, John Gribbin, in his 1993 book *In the Beginning:*

1. The Earth is a single living organism.
2. Each galaxy is also, literally, a living entity.
3. Our universe is also alive.
4. Our universe was once a "baby" universe in another universe.
5. Our living universe is seeding other baby universes through black holes.
6. The purpose of the universe is to create black holes.

None of this scientific proposal rests on any proven fact. Nor is it observable in practice or in principle; nor does it address the causation.

Enough said?

Or should I ask about the amount of faith it requires to believe in these alternative theories?

You may recall the Vatican conference where Pope John Paul II addressed the cosmologists and challenged them on the implications of the beginning of the universe.

Stephen Hawking's solution, despite all his work on black holes, is to find a way to make the beginning not really a beginning.

Hawking used that very same Vatican conference to introduce to the world his now-famous "no-boundary" theory of the universe.

In the Hartle-Hawking no-boundary universe—Hawking refined his original theory with fellow scientist Jim Hartle—our universe exists within a larger superspace made of real and mathematically imaginary time. Here, time is not linear, but more like a sphere. Choosing a beginning point in this "sphere" of real and imaginary time would be impossible, just as it would be impossible to choose that our planet begins at, say, the south pole.

In other words, this universe has a finite size but no boundaries to mark space and time.

Size, but no boundaries?

In his book *A Brief History of Time,* Hawking does point out what should already be obvious: This is only a principle that cannot be deduced from another principle.

In other words, it is only speculation.

Patrick Glynn, author of *God: The Evidence,* nails it on the head when he says "the mainstream scientific community has in effect shown its attachment to the atheistic ideology of the random universe to be in some respects more powerful than its commitment to the scientific method itself."

Just as the church reluctantly let go of false science centuries earlier, perhaps it is time for the scientific community to reexamine its own cherished beliefs.

11

The Six Days
of Genesis

On the seventh day, having finished his task,
God rested from all his work.

GENESIS 2:2

Skeptics may well look at the evidence of the anthropic principle and the big bang and decide there is good reason to believe that God is the Creator of our universe.

Yet strictly speaking, science that points us toward God tells us nothing about the nature of God, our own souls, good and evil, or the existence of an afterlife. These issues are dealt with in the most magnificent book in human history, the Bible, with its creation account.

Much as reason helps, faith in this God takes, well, a step of faith. There is great comfort, however, in knowing that the anthropic principle and the big bang indicate the foundational claim of the Bible to be true.

Genesis is the only ancient creation account to tell us that our universe was created. All the others speak of an eternal universe.

Readers of Genesis will note that the creation account simply tells us that God—a supernatural being outside of the realm of nature and beyond our comprehension—was the causation of this universe.

Genesis does not tell us how God did it, except that it was a creation. Literally, something from nothing.

Which describes the scientific evidence provided by the big bang.

In short, science has brought us to a point where the question is not whether this universe was created, but how.

Among the many remarkable things about the Genesis account is how closely it describes the *order* of creation as validated by science:

Genesis 1:1-5: God created the universe. Light is separated from the dark.

Science: Creation began with the big bang. Light is literally formed as the universe cools enough for electrons to bond to nuclei, and radiation can move outward unimpeded.

Genesis 1:6-10: God forms the heavenly firmaments as the waters separate, and dry ground appears.

Science: Gravity causes material to clump together, the galaxies form, and so does our solar system. The earth cools, and water appears.

Genesis 1: 11-13: God brought into existence the first plant life on Earth.
Science: Water allows the existence of bacteria and algae and subsequent plant life.

Genesis 1:14-19: God caused the sky to show the bright lights of the heavenly bodies.
Science: Photosynthesis produces an oxygen-rich atmosphere that becomes transparent enough for light to pass through.

Genesis 1:20-23: God filled the waters, then the air with animal life.
Science: Animals appear in the oceans; winged insects appear above water and land.

Genesis 1: 24-25: God called forth the animals of land.
Science: From the animals of the ocean come the animals of the land.

Genesis 26-27: God created man.
Science: At the very pinnacle of all the events that began with the big bang, man appears in the universe to marvel at it and question its existence.

Mohammed Heydari-Malayeri and NASA

Hubble Telescope picture of a nearby massive star cluster

It has taken the last five centuries and all our modern technology to produce the scientific picture of the order of creation. How did the ancients who gave us Genesis already know it so well and so accurately?

Even as the Genesis account appears to be backed by science, some will find doubts because of the often difficult discussion/dispute over the time line of creation. Especially with the slow process of evolution, even if this is an evolution directed by God.

Did God—as Genesis tells us—finish with all of creation in six days to rest on the seventh?

Conventionally, there are two camps regarding the six days of Genesis—those who believe each day was a literal 24-hour period, and those who believe each day represents an indefinite period of time.

The Bible does not tell us how long these time periods were.

And frankly, how important is that question against the far more profound knowledge that we were created?

Nor does the Bible discuss evolution. (It doesn't mention dinosaurs, but neither does it mention bananas or oranges.)

The Bible's worldview is very simple. God created this world and us. This is not in conflict with science. It *is* in conflict with a naturalistic worldview that tells us God did not have a part in creation.

Now, entering the twenty-first century, the more we learn in science, the more difficult it seems to support a naturalistic worldview.

And the easier it is to accept the Genesis account as a mysteriously wonderful account of our beginnings.

Some note that the description of time in the Bible can be divided into two categories: the first six days, and all the time thereafter.

Biblical historical events described by the time "thereafter" have been proven remarkably accurate by archaeologists, just as the unfolding of the first six days has been validated by science.

In his book *The Science of God,* author Gerald L. Schroeder presents an interesting hypothesis. He first notes:

> The opening chapter of Genesis acts like the zoom lens of a camera. Day by day it focuses with increasing detail on less and less time and space. The first day of Genesis encompasses the entire universe. By the third day, only Earth is discussed. After day six, only that line of humanity leading to the patriarch Abraham is in biblical view. The Bible realizes that the entire universe exists. But its interest now rests solely on one line of humanity. This narrowing of perspective, in which each successive day presents in greater detail a smaller scope of time and space, finds a parallel in scientific notation.

Schroeder, who is an applied theologian with undergraduate and doctoral degrees from the Massachusetts Institute of Technology, goes on to discuss Einstein's theory of relativity, a description of how changes in gravity or changes in velocity affect the rate at which time flows. (If you were traveling at close to the speed of light, for example, two minutes passing for you might take two thousand years to pass for the rest of us on Earth.)

Schroeder notes that our earthly perspective looks back from the present and surveys the billions of years it took for the unfolding of creation. But the Bible's perspective is one that looks *forward* from the beginning moment of time. Given this premise, and the demonstrable truth in Einstein's theory, Schroeder makes a good mathematical argument that each perspective supports the other within the first six days of creation.

In the end, the most important question concerns not the process of creation, but the origin.

The most profound implication is this: If God created this universe, this Earth, and finally, humans with souls, each of us is on an incredible eternal journey.

It is our task to be searchers for the truths behind this journey.

12
Fatherhood

For the scientist who has lived by his faith in the power of reason, the story ends like a bad dream. He has scaled the mountains of ignorance; he is about to conquer the highest peak; as he pulls himself over the final rock, he is greeted by a band of theologians who have been sitting there for centuries.

ROBERT JASTROW, ASTRONOMER

I have come to fatherhood relatively late in life. Over the months it has taken to write this book, I have had the joy of watching my baby daughter learn to walk, to experiment with sounds, to chase after our kittens. And now, she is almost ready to talk.

Some nights, in the darkness when she sleeps, I lean down and put my ear against her chest. I love the smell of her skin and hair. I love the sound of her breathing. And I love to listen to the beat of her little heart.

According to the classical laws of relativity and cosmology, we should not exist. Nor this planet. Nor the sun. Nor any matter in the universe.

When energy converts to mass, according to Einstein's famous $E=mc^2$, particles form into pairs—quarks and antiquarks. (Protons and neutrons, the nuclei of elements, are formed of quarks.) Quarks and antiquarks are identical to each other in most aspects, but when one touches the other, each explodes, and in a burst of energy, self-annihilates. Thus mass (m) converts back to energy (E).

In the first moments of creation, the energy levels were so high that immediately upon self-destruction, new quarks and antiquarks were formed. But as the tiny universe began to cool, there was no way for new quarks and antiquarks to replace the destroyed ones.

(If antimatter sounds like science fiction, you may find it interesting to know that it was discovered and observed in 1932 by a scientist at Caltech, and has been generated in particle accelerators since 1952.)

What *should* have happened is that all matter should have been exploded by antimatter. No matter should have survived anywhere; this universe should have merely become space with a weak radiation below the energy of a single microwave oven.

Instead, inexplicably, for every ten billion antiquarks, the beginning universe created ten billion and one quarks. This infinitesimal excess of matter became the planets, stars, and galaxies of the universe.

Because of this, *Scientific American* posed this question in a 1993 issue: "How is it that so much matter managed to survive?...Why is there something rather than nothing?"

Science cannot give us that answer.

When I listen to the beat of my daughter's heart, a great, quiet love fills me. I do not say this because this sense of love is unique to me. What is incredible is that each of us as parents are given a unique sense of it.

Of all the human loves, I believe this parent-child love can be the purest. I do not love my daughter because of what I can gain from the love, but because of what it allows me to give.

From where does love come?

How is it that something so invisible is so strong?

Roger Penrose, the renowned Oxford mathematician, estimated the likelihood of the physics constants producing the conditions and energy distribution at the moment of creation in such a way that the universe would eventually support life. The chances, he calculated, were less than one in 10^{123}. That is a 10 followed by 123 zeros.

Sometimes, in the dark, with my head softly against my daughter's chest, a haunting sadness will overcome me.

I hope that she will love me as much as I love her.

I hope, too, that I will live until I am old. That I will watch her grow into a woman, that I will one day hold her son or daughter the way I once held her.

Listening to my baby's heartbeat, I think of how growing old will take me toward my death. My love for her, and her love for me, will not be able to turn away that certainty.

So will come the day when, perhaps, she lays her head against my own chest to listen to the frail thumping of a heart close to its final beat.

This is the great sadness that comes with the great joy of love.

Somehow, for every ten billion antiquarks, the universe created ten billion and one quarks.

Somehow, against the odds of $\frac{1}{10}^{123}$, the universe grew in such a way to make life possible on Earth.

Incredible as this is, it is too easy to get lost in the abstractions of what science tells us about creation.

In trying to understand how this universe was not a random event, what matters most to me is listening to the heartbeat of my daughter.

I exist, as does she, because our bodies are composed of the dust of the stars. The carbon and hydrogen and oxygen and trace elements are arranged in such a way that we breathe, that our eyes interpret light waves, that our brain, in a mysterious manner, generates thoughts and gives instructions to our bodies.

What an amazing, incredible process.

Is it so preposterous to think that this world is moved by an invisible hand, that something or someone created it and exists beyond what we can sense?

NASA and Space Telescope Science Institute

Star clusters born in the wreckage of cosmic collisions

We are made of ancient stardust.

But it is more than that, more than the interplay of the four forces of physics that allow atoms and molecules to exist as they do.

My daughter, like me, had once been a pinpoint of protein known as DNA, growing into a complex organism according to the preprogrammed direction of that DNA. I have marveled to watch her grow, sustained by proteins and carbohydrates and water.

More than that, we all are sustained because of the sunlight—not too strong, not too weak—from a star the perfect distance away from Earth. This sunlight has allowed plants to grow in the dirt that had once been stardust. Not only do our bodies depend on these plants, we find nutrition in the protein of animals that eat these plants.

The life cycle on this planet exists because of sunlight and water and dirt, all possible because of the creation-events set in motion at the beginning of time. It's that simple. And that wonderfully profound.

Because we see it and live it everyday, we rarely give this process any thought.

Yes, on the one hand, it may sometimes seem preposterous to think of an invisible, supernatural Creator.

And on the other hand, when I hold my daughter and listen to her heartbeat in the night, I believe it is equally preposterous to imagine all this happening without one.

In his book *God: The Evidence,* Patrick Glynn compares modern science's discovery of the random universe to the "discovery" of America by Columbus. Because Columbus had been looking for Asia, he assumed it to be Asia. Later, as the exploration continued, it finally became clear it was not Asia at all, but a new and glorious continent.

I like his analogy.

Over the last several centuries, science has assumed ours to be a random universe, and with this predetermination has not seen it in any other way. In fairness to this assumption, up until very recently, a person of reason would have reviewed the evidence of science and had cause to agree with atheists.

But now that science has begun to explore more and more of the universe, it is covering more territory than ever expected.

Now it looks more and more like the sun that dawns on this new continent is one set in motion by a Creator.

In the end, however, God does not speak to me in science.

Yes, I welcome what I've learned through science, for it strengthens the ability of my intellect to accept His existence.

Where I am able to listen and understand God is when I listen to the beat of my daughter's heart, when I see that invisible, immeasurable something that exists apart from atoms and molecules and gravity and the explosion of the big bang and the causation of the universe.

In His gift of love.

6-30-01

About Michael Carroll
and his Astronomical Paintings

Michael W. Carroll has been an astronomical artist for 20 years and has done commissioned work for NASA and the Jet Propulsion Laboratory. His art has appeared in several hundred magazines throughout the world, including *National Geographic, Time, Asimov's Science Fiction, Smithsonian, Astronomy, Analog, Harper's, Ciel et Espace,* Japan's *Newton,* and *Sky & Telescope.* His paintings have aired on *Nova, National Geographic Explorer, Cosmos,* and various TV specials, and have embellished record albums and numerous books, including works by Carl Sagan, Arthur C. Clarke, David Brin, Terence Dickinson, and publications by Zondervan, Cook, Time-Life, Moody, Bantam, and others. He has exhibited works at the Smithsonian Air and Space Museum, at Moscow's Institute of Space Research (IKI), NASA Headquarters in Washington, D.C., the Reuben H. Fleet Science Center, and he has had traveling exhibits throughout the world. One of his paintings has flown aboard Russia's *Mir* space station in 1995, and another aboard Russia's ill-fated Mars 96 mission. Recent murals include the Denver Museum of Natural History, Fleet Science Center in San Diego, and Michigan's Longway Planetarium.

Carroll is a Fellow of the International Association for the Astronomical Arts and a member of the NASA Arts Program, and was an invited participant on a U.S. Geological Survey expedition to the Bering Glacier in Alaska, where he did paintings for a Survey-sponsored art exhibition which traveled throughout the United States.

You can contact Michael Carroll at www.spacedinoart.com or by telephone: (303) 933-1645.

Notes

1. Dava Sobel, *Galileo's Daughter* (New York: Viking, 1999), p. 65.
2. Nearly 400 years later, Pope John Paul II endorsed a commission-finding that declared the church's mistake in condemning Galileo.
3. A portion of an essay from my Mars Diaries series.
4. Fred Hoyle, *The Origin of the Universe and the Origin of Religion* (Wickford, RI: Moyer Bell, 1994).
5. These are just a few constants in physics at the atomic level that make the universe possible for life. This list goes on and on. For a comprehensive list, read *Universes* by John Leslie (London: Routledge, 1989).
6. Charles Colson, *How Now Shall We Live?* (Carol Stream, IL: Tyndale House Publishers, 1999), p. 59.
7. Quoted from Denys Wilkinson, *Our Universes* (New York: Columbia University Press, 1991), pp. 188-189.

118

origin of grief

DISTORTION of religion

A. man made DISTORTION

B. SATANIC VIRUS/ Taken captive at

5C predictable unchangeable

(C immutable Remain Unchanged

ⓒ The Prophets/ abraham Heschel 298